WAITING
with BRANDO

PLANNING A PARADISE IN TAHITI

by Bernard Judge

ORO editions
Publishers of Architecture, Art, and Design
Gordon Goff – Publisher and Art Director
USA, ASIA, EUROPE, MIDDLE EAST
www.oroeditions.com
info@oroeditions.com

Copyright © 2011 by ORO *editions*

ISBN: 978-0-9826226-4-3

Designed by Sara Pastrana
Production by Usana Shadday and Gabriel Ely
Project Coordinator: Christy LaFaver
Color Separation and Printing: ORO Group Ltd.
Printed in China

Library of Congress Cataloging-in-Publication Data Available.

ORO editions has made every effort to minimize the overall carbon footprint of this project. As part of this goal, ORO editions, in association with Global ReLeaf, have arranged to plant two trees for each and every tree used in the manufacturing of the paper produced for this book. Global ReLeaf is an international campaign run by American Forests, the nation's oldest nonprofit conservation organization. Global ReLeaf is American Forests' education and action program that helps individuals, organizations, agencies, and corporations improve the local and global environment by planting and caring for trees.

North American Distribution:

Publishers Group West / Perseus
1700 Fourth Street
Berkeley, CA 94710
USA
www.pgw.com

International Distribution:
www.oroeditions.com

For Blaine

PROLOGUE

Passports. They tell a lot about you and miss a lot as well. While rummaging about a shelf looking for some #2 drafting pencils, I ran across a small brown box, beat up at the corners and held together with masking tape. It looked familiar, but I couldn't remember what I had put in it. Passports, it turned out, a bunch of them: eleven, counting one of my mother's. The rest were mine.

The first was issued in 1935: Bernard Judge, citizen of the United States; Height: three feet zero inches; Hair: blond; Eyes: blue; Distinguishing marks or features: none; Place of birth: New York, NY; Date of birth: June 9, 1931; Occupation: XXX. A photograph of a very happy-looking, four-year-old boy in a sailor suit put a face on the data. There is a notation, penned carefully in red ink, that reads: "This passport is not valid for travel in Spain or for travel to or in any foreign state in connection with entrance into or service in foreign military or naval forces." Whoever wrote that must have thought that Generalissimo Franco was in dire need of little sailors.

Six pages of visas follow. Port entries are mostly to France, but also to Mexico, Guatemala, Panama, and Nicaragua, right up to 1938. I don't remember these trips except that I was on the decks of ships and on a leash most of the time to keep me from falling overboard. I do recall things about living in Nicaragua, though. That's where I first went to school–a German school. My American father, an architect who was working on the Capitol Building in Managua, thought it was "cleaner" than other schools. My fondest memory is of Juana, my governess, with her long, braided, shiny black hair. She loved me like her own. I remember traveling by train from Nicaragua to Mexico with my French mother, an amateur anthropologist and painter. In Mexico City, I continued my studies in another German school. My father had left my mother and me in Central America to go to work on the design of the 1939 World Fair in New York.

My second passport was issued in 1939, in Paris, France. This was not my first time in France, though. I had traveled frequently on my mother's passport to visit my grandparents. The photograph in this document shows a serious young boy in a seersucker jacket, with slicked-down hair. My mother must have done that. The passport also states that I cannot enter into foreign military service. This time it is stamped in red. Since I was now eight years old, the limitation made a little more sense, but really, just a little. My passport shows that I left France in July 1939, before the Germans invaded. I remember bits of those days: hearing Hitler's ranting on the radio, playing in the pebbled gardens of the Palace of Fontainebleau, and collecting delicious girolle mushrooms in the forest with my grandfather.

My third passport was issued in Casablanca, French Morocco, in 1954. How I got to Morocco without a passport is a bit of a mystery. I had finished high school in Forest Hills, New York, had worked for the architects of the United Nations Building, and joined the U.S. Navy in 1950. They put me in the Sea Bees and sent me to Morocco. I guess they didn't issue passports to servicemen in those days. Since I had refused a free passage home from Morocco, compliments of the Navy, they probably just said, "Now you're on your own, buddy." I must have gone to the American Embassy in Casablanca to request a passport. The photo this time shows a young man with a military crew cut and a slightly bewildered expression. It reports that I am six feet tall and a student. Countries in which the passport is not valid include Albania, Bulgaria, China, Czechoslovakia, Hungary, Poland, Romania, and the Union of Soviet Socialist Republics. Now that I was actually of military age, the passport reads I am "not to enter into the service of a foreign military." Finally it made sense.

I spent three and a half years in Morocco. While there, I traveled extensively in the Sahara, to Mauritania, Algeria, and Tangier, where I lost my virginity to an exotic cabaret dancer I fell madly in love with. I was fascinated by the architecture, the people, the colors, the cuisine, fragrances, and music of Morocco. I took up photography and when my time was up in the Navy, I stayed in North Africa until my discharge pay ran out. After six months, I hitch-hiked through

Spain and on to Paris, where I enrolled in the Beaux Arts School of Architecture and spent most my time trying to get work as a photographer. That year in Paris was the best year of my life: the bistros, the boulevards, the occasional fashion photo shoot, and meeting friends in the neighborhood café for white wine at breakfast. It was cheaper than coffee.

My fourth passport was issued in 1958 in Los Angeles, where I was attending the University of Southern California School of Architecture. The passport photograph shows a young fellow, looking self-assured and pleased with himself, dressed in a coat and tie. I note that I must have grown one half-inch, but still have no "distinguishing marks or features." Added to the countries for which the passport is not valid are the portions of China, Korea, and Vietnam that were under Communist control. Once again I am forbidden to enter into the service of a foreign state. The official stamps record travel to the Netherlands, Belgium, Germany, Switzerland, Italy, and France. While still in school, I had fallen in love with a beautiful ceramics major named Dora DeLarios. We got married and this was our first trip to Europe, where we stayed in campgrounds and traveled everywhere on a scooter.

Passport number five was issued in 1962, again in Los Angeles. The photographer caught me with a half smile and a quizzical look. The same old countries are excluded, and Cuba is added to the list. Now, the passport states that a person who travels to or in the listed countries is "liable to prosecution." Not a peep, however, about my not being able to join a foreign army.

This particular passport has twelve additional pages glued to the back. They accordion out to accommodate added visas, and entry and exit stamps. 1962 was the year Dora and I had taken a year off and knap-sacked around the world. Our passports prohibited us from entering Cambodia, but determined to see the ruins of Angkor Wat, we climbed over a barbed-wire fence and just snuck in – and later, out again. Our most profoundly moving experience on the trip was camping in the game parks of East Africa. The landscapes were stunning. I had a visceral connection with the animals that we encountered in the wild. When we returned to Los Angeles, we were changed people, and penniless.

In 1965 our daughter Sabrina arrived (without a passport).

The photo in my next passport, issued in 1966, has me looking slightly crazed, a look many new fathers share. Entering certain countries can still result in "prosecution." The pages of visas and entry stamps remind me that our family visited my grandmother in France, and stopped along the way in England and Denmark. I also took a side trip to Berlin, which, at the time, was behind the "iron curtain." In 1969, there is a stamped entry to Faaa, Tahiti, from my very first trip to French Polynesia. I remember that airport clearly. Over time I would become very familiar with it. But I didn't know that then.

The seventh passport, issued in 1971, has an interesting notation: "U.S. courts have interpreted U.S. law as not restricting the travel of U.S. citizens to any foreign country"; however, "travel to Cuba,

China, North Korea and North Vietnam is authorized only when validated by the Department of State." At least the list of countries is a bit shorter. I still have an earnest smile, and look decently professional in my seersucker jacket and tie. I note that I have gone to France, probably for my grandmother's funeral, and that I have been in and out of Tahiti eleven times between '71 and '74.

In 1977, the passport is a smaller document and, for the first time, has no travel restrictions. I have gained some weight, have a receding hairline, slightly graying at the temples, and I am now wearing a corduroy jacket instead of that old seersucker coat. Flipping through the pages, I find that I have made seven trips to Tahiti.

My personal information and photograph are entirely encased in plastic in my 1982 passport. I am now fifty years old, wearing a button-down shirt, tie, and tweed jacket. I count thirty-two trips to Tahiti and one trip to France. I went by myself.

The tenth passport was issued in Los Angeles in 1987. I look my age in the photo. I have more forehead than hair. I am wearing a polo shirt and I'm back to that same old seersucker jacket. I see fifteen trips to Tahiti, and one to New Zealand and Australia. I had been researching the environmental problems associated with building on islands, particularly on coral reefs, at the Great Barrier Reef. I also note that a client of mine sent me to Samoa, another to Bali.

Ten are a lot of passports. Just for fun, and to remind myself where I've been during the ensuing years, I get out my most recent passport, number eleven. My neck has by now turned into jowls. I am wearing the old corduroy jacket. There are thirteen trips to Tahiti so far, and one to Fiji.

In 1998, I renewed an old friendship with Blaine Mallory, a woman I had met many years ago in Los Angeles. We fell in love and went to France and Spain together, and yes, to Tahiti. We married in 2001 and since then have visited parts of Mexico, Bali, the jungles of Guatemala, the Mekong, and the Andes.

Passports, and the pictures in them, tell a lot about a person, but they do not tell the whole story.

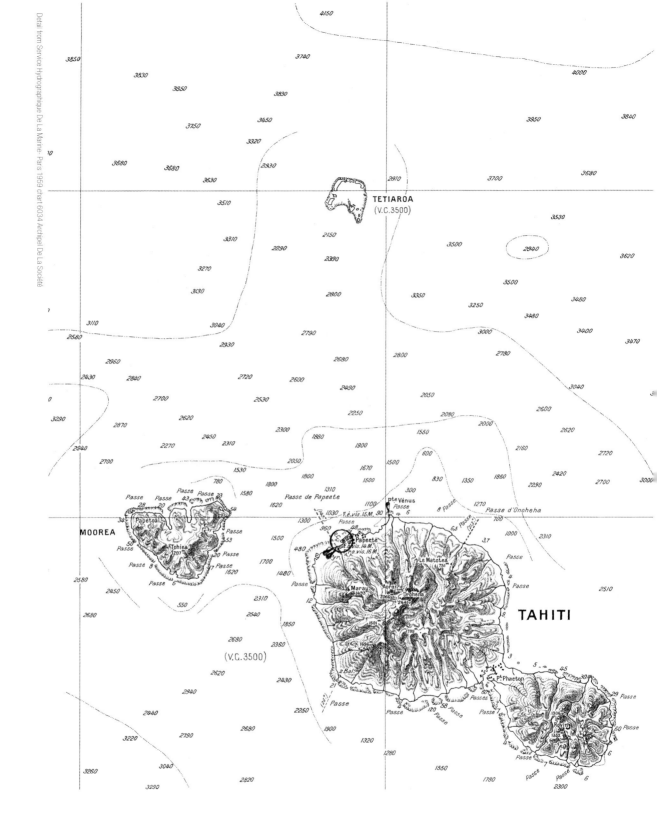

The high islands of Tahiti and Moorea in the South Pacific.
Moorea is 13 miles, and Tetiaroa Atoll is 32 miles, from Papeete Harbor.

THE BEGINNING

A Dangerous Approach
Ghosts and Tikis

I found myself happily skipping over whitecaps formed by the Westerly trades, surveying the endless, deep-blue South Pacific, squinting expectantly at the horizon. It had been almost three hours on a fast but small fishing boat with my wife Dora, our rotund Tahitian skipper Captain Siki, and an even larger Tahitian sailor whose name I have since forgotten. I was exhilarated, standing on the foredeck with the spray in my face, inhaling the salty smells of the sea and feeling the brilliant sun on my shoulders.

It was still early morning. We had left the island of Moorea at dawn, and the light on the ocean was gleaming and bright. We strained our eyes looking for a slight blue haze on the horizon, a sailor's marker of landfall. And there it was, in the distance, due north from Tahiti. Birds circled low above the sea, but before they had a chance to point the way, palm trees appeared, dancing on the water. It was a truly astonishing sight. Just a short time later, we could detect the bright white of crashing waves, the sign of a barrier reef protecting an atoll, its inner lagoon, and the islands within.

I carried with me a letter of introduction written by Marlon Brando's secretary, Alice Marshak. As our boat approached the reef, I fully expected to be met by a flotilla of canoes carrying native girls bedecked in flowers, steered by strong tattooed paddlers who would take me to Marlon. But as we got closer, I was dismayed to discover that there was no welcoming party at all. In fact, there was no movement whatsoever on the beach beyond the reef. Completely taken aback and discouraged to have arrived at what appeared to be a deserted island, but curious, I decided to go in by myself, without Dora. Siki cut the engine and motioned for me to prepare to go ashore. But how? We had no canoe, no skiff.

The Tahitian sailor donned his mask and fins, and dove overboard with his spear fishing gear in hand. Swallowing a lump in my throat, I took off my shirt, tied my sneakers to the belt of my swimsuit, tucked Alice's letter into a corner of my mask, grabbed my fins, and slipped into the ocean behind him. Mask gone quickly askew, letter in one eye, shoes bobbing, I treaded water frantically, trying to get myself organized. I could scarcely believe where I was: in an enormous expanse of ocean, 50 yards from the shore of a tiny island in the middle of nowhere, with the boat that had delivered me sailing swiftly away to go fishing, and with my wife aboard! Once I recovered my bearings, I tried to follow my guide, who was swimming smoothly toward the reef. Apparently it had not occurred to our captain that a *popaa* (a white foreigner) like me might not be a strong ocean swimmer, let alone know anything about crossing coral reefs. Coral reefs are massive, wide, irregular walls rising from the depths of the ocean to just above the surface; they are jagged formations that look soft and porous, but are actually hard as concrete, with razor-sharp edges, clefts, and crevices.

Being submerged in the ocean outside a reef, waves crashing overhead, is not for the faint-hearted. When viewed from above, the ocean has texture, color, movement; it is hypnotic, but it lacks an essential dimension. When viewed from within, the ocean unveils its unfathomable depth. It is at times opaque, at times clear, and reveals a dimension of density. It is also full of life. For me, that morning, the experience was overwhelming – the seemingly bottomless void below, all manner of large fish swimming around me. I knew I had to focus. I swam slowly toward the emerging reef ahead. It reminded me of flying low in an airplane, approaching mountains with steep and rugged valleys, sloping gently upward towards the white clouds, which, all of a sudden, turn into angry thunderstorms. Powerful waves forced me toward bubbling foam crashing on a coral reef. I was scared out of my wits. As the reef became just within reach, I was pulled away from it by a receding wave. Back and forth I went, until I was able to grab the edge of the reef; but as I tried to hoist myself up onto it, I was pulled back again by another wave. Each time I got a little further onto the reef, but I could not compete with the force of the waves. The thought struck me that this was serious and I was insane to be there. I was in trouble. I might actually die. At last, a large hand got a hold of my hair and pulled me to a standing position. I was battered but safe, upright on that coral reef. I had never even seen one before, much less actually stood on one. My companion had surely saved my life. Staring at me, he shook his head in disgust and disappeared into the lagoon.

Feeling the pounding surf through my bones, I stood there, disoriented, shaken and unsteady on my feet, but dazzled by the sight of a placid, shimmering lagoon inside the reef. It took a while to gather my strength. My sneakers were lost, my bathing suit torn, but I was very much alive. Looking down, I saw that my chest, legs, arms, and hands were covered with blood from coral cuts. They hurt like hell, but before long, due to the sun, the bleeding stopped. Staring down at the fins still on my feet and the mask and snorkel dangling around my neck, I realized that my letter of introduction was gone. So was my Tahitian escort. It occurred to me that I was getting badly sunburned as well.

I was a little dazed, but I knew I couldn't stay on the reef all day, and so, holding my breath, I jumped into the lagoon. The bite of the salt water on the cuts was painful, but the cooling effect of the water was a welcome relief. It was only a short distance to the sandy beach, and the shade of the coconut trees beckoned. I tumbled ashore exhausted, lay down on the sand, stared up at the clear blue sky, and closed my burning eyes.

When I awoke, my eyes adjusted to the blinding blue sky framed by silhouettes of dark-green palm fronds sparkling with the reflection of the sun on their quivering leaves. It was a boyhood dream come true! Was it, in fact, a dream? There was not a footprint in sight anywhere on the pristine sand. The warm, moist air renewed my sense of reality as the soft tropical breeze stimulated me. I marveled at the clear, transparent waters of the lagoon, the colorful tropical fish darting among fantastically shaped coral heads, and the hermit crabs scurrying about trying to find new homes in abandoned shells. It's hard to describe my feelings. The powerful sense of undisturbed nature was compelling. "God", I thought, "this is a magical place." Surprisingly, I felt at home. I knew in my gut that I wanted these views, these sensations, and this harmony of limpid lagoons, brilliant white sand, swaying palms, and bright azure sky to be part of my life.

Wandering into a jungle of palms and vines set back from the beach, I came upon what looked like an abandoned village set among mango, breadfruit, and large sheltering shade trees. Decrepit cement block buildings with tin roofs, and broken screen doors and windows stood in the high grass. Everything was beyond repair, rotting and rusting away. Someone had lived there and left, perhaps in a hurry. Only lizards, rats, and crabs remained. Old cots, bedding, and mosquito netting had been left behind. Pots and rusty enameled metal dishes with Chinese designs were strewn about. It was all very mysterious. I was eager to learn more.

I struggled through the sharp, prickly brush and fallen trees to the other side of the island, where, across the wide lagoon, I was awed by the thousands of sea birds circling overhead and swooping into the foliage of a small islet about a mile in the distance. I could make out four or five tiny islands within the lagoon, and I was tempted to swim to each, making discoveries, but thought better of it, remembering my cuts and bruises.

Clearly, Marlon Brando was not there that day. No one at all lived there anymore. Had the letter of introduction I'd carried in my face mask been some kind of gag? Did Marlon Brando really want me to visit his uninhabited island? Me, an architect he'd never even met? Dora and I were always ripe for adventure, and thought it would have been fun to meet the infamous actor on his Polynesian island. If the letter was indeed a gag, it certainly was a costly one. It had nearly cost me my life. But truthfully, I thought every moment on the atoll was worth the dangers of getting there. I hoped that Dora, out on that fishing boat, was enjoying herself as much as I.

Before I knew it, dusk had fallen, and the boat that had dropped me off that morning materialized outside the reef. My Tahitian friend suddenly appeared in the lagoon, trailing a ribbon of fish he had caught during the day. He waved to me to join him as he headed back to the reef. I didn't want to leave that magical world, but light was fading, and it was getting late. Re-entering the water, I was again all too aware of the coral cuts stinging my body. The salt in the wounds reminded me of the dangers ahead and I approached the reef with trepidation. Once I had managed to climb onto the reef, I waited to see what would happen. Captain Siki held off, and after a series of waves had washed over the reef, my Tahitian friend signaled me to approach the edge and to dive into the waves as they receded. I held my breath, maneuvered to get close to the edge by walking backwards in my flippers, and dove in just as a wave began to wash away. This time, swimming as hard as I possibly could so as not to be caught by the next incoming wave, I made it to Siki's boat, gratefully unhurt.

Once aboard, Captain Siki and the sailor lay me down on the deck, sat on my feet, and held my head as they proceeded to rub fresh limes on my open wounds. I screamed to high heaven until Dora, bless her soul, poured rum down my throat. If it had not been for the rum, I'm sure that I would have passed out. We learned afterward that fresh lime juice is a Tahitian remedy for coral cuts. Coral are microscopic organisms that can't distinguish the body's salty fluids from the environment of the sea. They might have stayed alive, grown, and festered in my body if it were not for the lime juice that had killed them. My life had been saved for the second time that day. Captain Siki's boat returned to Moorea that evening with one happy drunk with a once-in-a-lifetime memory.

Top
Sighting Tetiaroa for the first time.

Bottom
The beach is stunning — not a footprint to be seen.

Top
I find a deserted village...

Bottom
and islands in the lagoon.

This story actually begins when Dora surprised me with plane tickets to the islands of Tahiti, in French Polynesia. The two of us and our five-year-old daughter, Sabrina, were to spend Christmas and New Year's of 1969/70 at the Club Med Moorea. This was about as far away from my architectural firm in Los Angeles as she could get me. We did not know it at the time, but this was to be the beginning of an adventure that would change our lives.

By sheer chance, shortly before leaving Los Angeles for Moorea, I met a contractor named Jack Bellin, who was working for Marlon Brando at his Beverly Hills home. Jack was a handsome, robust fellow with whom I got along well right away. We had a similar spirit of adventure. Upon learning that I was going to Tahiti, he told me I had to visit Tetiaroa, Brando's private atoll. He said it was extraordinarily beautiful and secluded, a rare experience that would be well worth my while. It was Jack who had arranged the letter from Brando's secretary, giving me permission to visit the island.

I had heard of Tahiti, of course, but really knew nothing of French Polynesia. Reading a bit, I found that it covers a vast area of the south Pacific Ocean and consists of some 130 islands. I learned that its major groupings are the Society Islands, the Marquesas, the Tuamotus, and the Gambiers. The Societies are made up of the Windward Islands — including Tahiti and its near neighbor Moorea, where we would be staying — and the Leeward Islands, the most famous of which is Bora Bora. Legendary Tahiti serves as the center of government for all of French Polynesia. It was ruled by the Pomare Dynasty until 1880, when it became a French Colony, and in 1957, a French overseas territory. To this day Tahiti depends on France for its economic well-being. Tahiti is located 4,000 miles from the West Coast of the United States, 2,800 miles south of Hawaii, 3,700 miles east of Australia, and 5,000 miles west of South America. In other words, it is smack in the middle of nowhere, far removed, in more ways than one, from the rest of the world.

Arriving in Tahiti in those days was great fun. There was virtually no tourism. The Club Med Moorea had just opened. Pan Am, UTA French Airlines, and Air New Zealand had just begun jet service, and the planes were usually only half full. The service was great. The airport at Faaa was an open-air building. You could simply walk through and greet family and friends, handing them anything that would normally have to be declared — before going through customs. Papeete, the Tahitian capital, was a typical South Seas waterfront town lined with shade trees. At the time, it was teeming with bicycles and scooters rather than automobiles. Bars and sidewalk cafes lined the waterfront. Huge cargo ships, local fishing vessels, and yachts from all over the world were moored along the wharf in the middle of "downtown." Papeete was known as a harbor safe from hurricanes, so there were always lots of sailboats of all shapes and sizes, from ridiculously small to ridiculously large.

Our trans-Pacific flight had arrived at 6:00 a.m. Immediately upon disembarking, we were overtaken by the aroma of flowers, particularly that of the pungent *tiare* that everyone, men as well as women, wore behind their ears or in their hair. The warm, humid, and scented air was intoxicating. To this day, whenever I get off a plane in Tahiti, I am overwhelmed by the sweet fragrance of the *tiare*.

Bound for the port of Papeete that morning, we boarded "le truck," a colorful flatbed truck with benches along its sides and down the middle. The roofs of all "les trucks" were too low for standing, and passengers were forced to straddle the middle bench. This made for a strange form of gymnastics while getting in and out. Canoes, pigs, and baggage were carried on the roof, and local music played loudly on speakers as we drove along. As there were no regular stops, people got on and off at will, and no one seemed to mind if the driver only progressed a few yards between stops. Upon boarding "le truck," every single passenger was greeted with "*ia orana*" or "*bonjour*." The warmth and camaraderie were catching. We really enjoyed our stay from the get-go.

The sun was just peeking over the top of the mountains as we arrived at the Papeete ferry dock. The ride from the airport had taken almost an hour. It wasn't the distance that had made it such a long ride, but the frequent stops. The small ferry, Keke II, was very much like a floating "le truck." It had benches along its deck for passengers and a flat roof for the passengers' belongings. We had a couple of hours' wait before leaving for Moorea. In my seersucker suit, Brooks Brothers shirt, and tie, I started feeling the heat as the sun rose over the harbor.

The port was just waking up. Fishermen were unloading their catch next to the ferry and carrying it on long poles to the market nearby. People were arriving at the ferry with bundles of fruit, old boxes bulging with who-knows-what, even outboard motors or an occasional pig. Streets along the quay were filling up with brown, bare-chested men dressed in shorts, and women with long, black, shiny hair flowing over their colorful *pareus* (sarongs) or long, high-necked colonial dresses. All walked or rode bicycles or scooters, some two to a seat. The men wore hats made with woven leaves, and everyone had a flower behind the ear. Some of the women sported *courones*, which are flowered wreath headdresses. With every inch the sun climbed into the sky, my suit, shirt, and tie felt more out of style and out of place. But the sights, smells, and commotion were enthralling. As a child during the 1930s, I had lived with my parents in Managua, Nicaragua, and Mexico City. And so, to me there was something very familiar and pleasing about the apparent chaos all around us in this tropical setting.

Finally my coat and tie came off, and I rolled up my sleeves. Dora and Sabrina wandered off to discover the open-air market, and I was relegated to minding the luggage — as if that was necessary. Boxes and packages were strewn all along the quay and no one touched anyone else's belongings. We had definitely left the urban world and all its ills behind us.

Only 13 miles to the west and two hours by ferry, Moorea is a high island. Like Tahiti, it is the remnant of an ancient volcano. Its jagged peaks and deep valleys are a spectacular sight, especially when approached by boat. We had already spent two wondrous hours at sea, albeit under the scorching sun, before arriving in Paopao Bay, also known as Cooks Bay, which must be the most picturesque bay in the world. After unloading at the dock next to the old Aimeo Hotel, we set off in "le truck" down the bumpy road to the Club Med. My face and arms had turned beet red from exposure to the elements. I don't know if it was the sun-sensitized skin of my arm next to the practically bare breast of the long-haired *vahine* next to me, or simply the animal contact of skin to skin in the tropics that overpowered me; whatever it was, I still remember that sensual feeling today.

Two weeks on Moorea was enough time for us to get to know the island pretty well. We visited archaeological sites, waterfalls, and high plateaus overlooking stunning bays. Life at the Club was great fun. Francois Tiger, our very energetic GO, "*gentil organisateur,*" or entertainment director, kept us busy and always amused. We went on picnics, watched neighborhood kids perform Tahitian dances, saw crazy shows put on by the staff, and danced to live drums and guitars on a pontoon in the lagoon. It seemed like we were up all night every night!

We made friends with several "Mooreans" that stayed at the Club, because there were few other places for locals to "get away" on the island. We met an English painter named Jean Shelsher on a Club Med diving excursion. Jean spent much of her life in Moorea, built her own studio in one of the picturesque valleys of the island, and has become one of the most well-respected watercolorists in Polynesia. When we met her, she was minding the Gump property on Moorea for the owner of Gump's Department Store in San Francisco.

Gump's house still sits high on a ridge overlooking Cooks Bay with the same fantastic panoramic view, not only of the Bay, but also the pass through the reef and the ocean beyond. The house stands alone to this day. Not many people would build a house on the precipitous mountains forming the Bay. As we entered Cooks Bay on our first day and spotted the Gump house with its thatch roof jutting out beautifully from the trees along the ridge, I remember thinking, "Now, that's how to live."

Dora and I met the "Bali Hai Boys," three young Californians who had recently opened a small bungalow-style hotel. Tourism was just beginning, and the boys were famous for greeting incoming passengers at the Faaa airport to try to steal them away from other hotels in Tahiti.

Top
The tuna fleet in Papeete Harbor,
late 1960s.

Bottom
"Le truck" at the marketplace,
late 1960s.

Top
Unloading a day's catch.

Bottom
Papeete Harbor in the early 1970s.

Top
A large ocean liner dwarfs the town of Papeete.

Left
Sport fishing boats similar to that of Captain Siki's.

Right
Tahitian mountains in the mist.

I was immediately taken by Tahiti's charm, its mountains, its people.

"Hey, come over to our place on Moorea. It's much more fun than the others and a lot cheaper too." They gave free rooms to the Pan Am crews who did a little promotion for them on the incoming flights. Their strategy worked, though they became unpopular with the French hotel owners in Tahiti. Imagine this kind of flagrant marketing campaign on a major airline today!

We met Pauline Teariki, the owner of the oldest pension on the island, Chez Pauline. She was in her seventies, the "grand dame" of Moorea, and a repository of ancient lore. She rented out two bedrooms in her old colonial house, which was situated next to a stream. Dining there was an experience; you'd be seated under vines and flaming bougainvillea on a rickety bridge over water swarming with mosquitoes. The well-worn veranda, lined with broken chairs and cracked window panes, was a remnant of times past, yet still warm and welcoming. Pauline's cuisine was a simple but excellent mixture of exquisite Tahitian and French tastes. Fresh fish was served in ginger sauces alongside exotic fruits and accompanied by fine French wines. But, oh my God, the mosquitoes! Pauline herself was pencil thin, with long gray hair braided down her back, her face lined with life's experiences. She had the beauty, bearing, voice, and countenance of a spiritual person, and she commanded respect without ever asking for it. She was pure Polynesian, while also deeply steeped in French culture.

Polynesia harbors many contradictions. At first, it seemed to me that the Polynesian people were perfectly content to live a simple life. They had abundant quantities of fish, fruit, and flowers, and most didn't have to work for a living. It took a while for me to realize that in fact, their lives were impeded by modern-day world culture. The Polynesian people had migrated from Southeast Asia and Indonesia over a 6,000-year period, the last between 300 and 900 AD. Slowly, they sailed and paddled from island to island across the Pacific and finally reached Easter Island to the east, Hawaii to the north, New Zealand to the south, and Fiji to the west. Polynesians and their culture were the last to be discovered by the Western world. It took until the late 18th century for Europeans to arrive. The Polynesians had time to develop their own distinctive language, Oceanic, distinctive seafaring techniques utilizing double-hulled outrigger sailing canoes, and methods of farming taro root, coconut, sugarcane, breadfruit, and bananas different even from those in Southeast Asia or South America. They also developed distinctive physical characteristics. Though it is rare today to find a pure Polynesian, it seems to me that when I am with a group of Tahitians, I recognize two very pronounced body types. One is tall and elongated like Pauline and the other short and round like Captain Siki. This "phenomenon" has always been striking to me, but given the amount of intermingling between Polynesians and Europeans immediately following the arrival of the latter in the late 18th century, it makes sense. This was the age of whaling and missionaries. Whaling, in particular, brought Europeans to Polynesia, many of whom stayed and "married," not always legally. The missionaries' concept of legal marriage was new to Polynesia, and took a while to be adopted, but it is not uncommon today for Tahitians to bear both Christian first names and European last names. Unfortunately, Europeans brought more than new concepts; they brought diseases. A ship's doctor from Captain Cook's Dolphin, one of the earliest European ships to arrive in Tahiti, noted that there was no natural immunity to venereal diseases among the local population. Within months, syphilis and gonorrhea spread like wild fire. White man and his virulent diseases were largely responsible, it is said, for cutting Tahiti's estimated population of 200,000 (Cook's estimate) to 50,000 within just a few years. Though the figures are in dispute, there is little doubt that the early contact with Europeans, and with whaling fleets, had a disastrous effect on the health of the Polynesian people. In 1918, after World War I, an influenza epidemic brought by returning soldiers virtually decimated the local population. Not only were diseases brought in by humans, but new plants, animals, and even flies also carried diseases.

At Pauline's, I discovered that some Tahitians believe in spirits, or *Tupapa'us*, which are people's souls that have come back from the dead, their lives on earth unfinished for some reason or other. They are not harmful or evil or mean. *Tupapa'us* are spirits who unexpectedly appear from time to time, particularly to people who are sensitive to the spiritual world and believe in the extraordinary. I have seen them myself. *Tupapa'us* float a few inches above the ground and simply watch. There is no reason to fear them. Surprisingly, it is those who do not believe in them who are most afraid of them.

Some Tahitians also believe in *tikis*. Pauline's front garden contained half a dozen of them. *Tikis* are ancient stone statues, carved in vaguely human form. They are squat figures without necks, and Tahitians are apt to believe they have supernatural powers. They can be either good *tikis* or bad *tikis*, but they are not the same as *tupapa'us*, who are ghosts who appear in human form. *Tikis* should never be moved, and if they are, they must be returned to their original location as soon as possible as, it is said, they can cast a terrible spell on those with the temerity to relocate them permanently. Needless to say, we always stepped around them with a certain amount of respect.

At the time, in 1969, the one road around Moorea was nothing more that a rutty coral track. When it rained, the mountain streams would wash out portions of the roadway and traffic would simply stop. There were never many cars, maybe a small truck or two, and most of the drivers would take the interruption not as an inconvenience, but as an opportunity to catch up on the latest gossip. This was referred to as the "coconut radio." Mind you, there were only 3,000 inhabitants on the island back then, mostly Tahitian, and everyone knew everyone else. Many of them, I'm sure, were probably somehow related. Moorea had a port in Cook's Bay where the ferry docked, but no real town; instead there were small villages made up of a Chinese store or two, and an occasional school and church. A small clinic not far from Chez Pauline served the island.

I vividly remember going on a marvelous tour around the island one day. The road ran

Top
A Tahitian house with a colonial touch.

Left
Dora and Sabrina having lunch at Chez Pauline.

Top
Cook's Bay (Pao Pao) in Moorea.

Right
Going to the Chinese store along Moorea's main road.

right along the beach. We stopped for lunch at a fantastic site: the beach, the mountains behind us, a view across the lagoon, the reef and the ocean, and Tahiti reigning gloriously in the distance. We sat there, eating loads of *poisson cru*, delectable raw fish swimming in coconut milk, washing them down with rum punches. Dora and I agreed that this was surely as good as life could be. When our holiday drew to a close, I resolved to make my way back as soon as I possibly could. I could hardly wait to return to Tetiaroa somehow, preferably without all the cuts and bruises I had drawn on my first trip. I knew I had to solve the mystery of that remarkable paradise and the famous man who owned it.

Nuupure, Moorea.

February 1970

A CLIENT

Discovering Brando
The Bars and Belles of Papeete

At the age of thirty-nine, I was already a confirmed workaholic. I've always loved being an architect. My work is my fun. The sheer pleasure of drawing that first black line on a blank sheet of white paper still gives me a thrill. Returning from the South Seas after New Year's, I couldn't wait to get back to my office. My associate, Ron Smart, had held down the fort, but there was a lot of catching up to do on various ongoing projects. I was ready to get back into the swing of things the moment I opened the door to the Schindler House on Kings Road in Hollywood. It was the first truly modern house built in Los Angeles, and I was lucky to have found it. Initially I shared half the house with Schindler's widow, Pauline. The house was built for two families with a shared kitchen, which was an idea for communal living written about by playwright George Bernard Shaw. I occupied Schindler's old studio, and Pauline occupied her half of the house. The house was, and still is, emblematic of a combination of shelter, technology, and social planning, all set in a verdant garden filled with bamboo stands, peach, avocado, fig, and orange trees.

My professional interests have always focused on the use of technology and industrial processes to solve construction and environmental problems. I am less interested in the architecture of artistic expression, or the design in the vogue of the day. To me, the architectural challenge is allowing an aesthetic to evolve out of the analysis of an architectural problem, not in imposing an aesthetic solution to the problem. For instance, in 1958, I built an experimental house in Southern California. The concept was to have people live in a garden, on platforms among trees and flowers, shielded from the elements by a transparent mylar skin and sunshade, suspended from a geodesic dome. The dome itself was Buckminster Fuller's first large-scale structure made of thin tubular aluminum struts, and was donated for the project. The bathroom, plug-in kitchen, and decks were assembled on a hillside site. The design was an effort to use recent technology to reduce the cost of construction. Dora and I lived in the house for a year and it continued to be inhabited for about ten years, after which time the mylar skin gave out and the house was dismantled. The dome was packed up and sent to the Smithsonian Institution in Washington, DC.

By that time I had conducted housing research in ten countries around the world. A structural system I designed had received a patent in 1966. In our spare time, Ron and I were building a house based on that system. If nothing else, by 1970, I had exhibited tenacity and resourcefulness on unusual projects. Consequently our office was quite busy, but that did not stop me from talking about Tahiti to anyone and everyone who would listen.

When we got back from the Club Med Moorea, I contacted Brando's contractor Jack in Beverly Hills. He had introduced me to Tetiaroa, I told him about my experiences getting there, which he received with peals of laughter. He knew that Marlon didn't know exactly what to do with his island and was searching for inspiration. I told him that sending people over the reef was certainly a strange way of doing that. I damn near lost my life. "Well, you decided to go over the reef; no one told you to, but I'm glad you survived and that you enjoyed the experience."

Jack himself was enthusiastic about the possibilities of development in Tahiti. He had been there a few years earlier, and had run across a beachfront property that he thought would make a good hotel site. As he was very busy at the time we spoke, he asked me if I would be interested in checking out the possibilities of the site for him. Despite the many projects going on in my own office, I jumped at the chance to return to Tahiti. I knew I was better qualified to take on this extraordinary job than Jack, for several different reasons: I spoke French fluently, and would therefore be able to speak with locals as well as officials and professionals. Jack agreed. He gave me a couple of names to look up, paid for my airline ticket, and handed me $1,000 in spending money. I often took chances to see if a project would develop, and this time, at least, I knew that it would be in a great location. If all went well with the site Jack had found, I was to be the architect, and he the developer. Within a month of having been there last, I was back on a plane heading for French Polynesia. Dora was not pleased to be left behind.

The plane left Los Angeles at midnight. They still do today. It is one of the very few things that have not changed over the years. French Polynesia is either two or three hours behind Los Angeles depending on the season, so after an eight-hour flight one arrives in Papeete early, ready for a full day of adventure, or in my case, a full day of work. I got off the plane so filled with excitement to be back, I could have burst.

On Jack's advice, I checked into the venerable Hotel Tahiti, right on the waterfront outside Papeete. Its main building had a thatched roof that was supported by carved coconut posts, a large reception area that opened to the sea, and an extra-long, shiny mahogany bar that was always occupied. As I entered the lobby, children were jumping off the pier in front of the hotel into the bay, screaming with delight. It could have been a movie set. There were almost no guests, just locals at the hotel bar, even that early in the morning; evidently, the bar was a good place to catch up on what was happening on the island. The rooms were just what one would expect in the tropics: airy, with louvered doors, screens for windows, expansive bathrooms with white tiles, fans slowly revolving overhead, and mosquito netting covering the beds. I remember feeling transported to another century, and I loved that feeling.

Carlos Palacios was the first person I was to look up from Jack's contact list. Carlos was Marlon's closest friend in Tahiti, a fine, elderly gentleman of the "old school". He was also the Chilean Consul. As a young man, he had been one of the first in Chile to earn a pilot's license, and he had traveled around the world. He was educated, had been groomed for the diplomatic corps, and had worked for the United Nations in New York. But he had been labeled the *bete noir* (black sheep) of his family after being posted to French Polynesia, where he was known to cavort with beautiful native girls. The final stroke for his wife and family back home was his open affair with a Tahitian girl. After that, his family disowned him, left him in Tahiti, and refused to deal with him ever again. I called Carlos on the phone in the hotel lobby. A local operator said he was not at home, but that she would try to find him. In those days, an operator would call around to find out who might know a person's whereabouts. I found this tracking system so innocent, and very human, very Tahitian, not to mention very helpful whenever I really needed to reach someone. The operator found Carlos at the Chinese store close to his house looking for his favorite Chilean wine. She would call me back when he returned. She told me that Agnes, Carlos' Tahitian *amie*, was at the beach with Teihotu, the boy she took care of. As I was soon to discover, Teihotu was Brando's son. Tahitian operators not only knew everyone who had a phone, but also their private business. When Carlos phoned back, he was delighted at the prospect of company from the U.S., and he invited me right over. Within an hour, I was on "le truck" off to Punaauia, 15 km from Papeete. The man at the hotel's front desk informed me that there were no street addresses in Tahiti. He told me to simply say to the driver, "PK 15—Carlos' house," and he would know exactly where to drop me off.

Carlos greeted me with warmth and oldworld charm. A small, thin, slightly fragile man, Carlos had an aristocratic bearing, sparkling eyes, and a shy smile. He was dressed in colonial style: long pants and a white, short-sleeved tailored shirt, worn loose over the belt. His simple living room was lined with books, photographs, and memorabilia from his many exploits all over the world. I explained my Tahitian "mission," and Carlos kindly offered to have Agnes show me the property Jack was interested in. Agnes was born and raised in French Polynesia, and like many Tahitians who are either Catholic or Protestant, had a Christian name. When Agnes appeared in her *pareu* through the hanging cowrie shells at the kitchen entry, I was immediately taken with her beauty, as well as her happy-go-lucky nature. She laughed and made jokes of practically everything anyone brought up. I could easily understand how this very lovely and amusing woman had seduced this refined man. She offered us fresh fruit and hot tea. "Tea in the tropics — how very European," I thought to myself.

During our conversation, Carlos asked if I was acquainted with his neighbor, Marlon Brando. When I replied that I knew of him, of course, but had never met him, he said, "Go on over there. He and Tarita live across from the Chinese store up the road, and he will be glad to meet you." I was excited to finally go to talk to the man who owned Tetiaroa, but didn't know what to expect. I had seen several of his films, and looked forward to meeting him, especially there, in beautiful "untouched" Tahiti, where the informality of the place would allow us to meet easily. I walked up the road and found the Chinese store and the house across the street. Like the others along the way there were no walls, fences, or gates, so I walked through the garden and the next thing I knew, I was entering the wide-open door of what could have been a white stucco California bungalow. "Hello," I called, "anybody home?" Out came a rather sturdy man, barefooted and pale-skinned with thinning grey-blond hair. His unmistakably familiar, expressive face was smiling broadly. He was dressed in a *pareu* over an impressive belly. "I'm Marlon," he said, exuding the casual friendliness so customary in Tahiti, "come on in." One thing about meeting movie actors: they look different in reality than they do on the screen. Marlon Brando was a lot shorter than I had envisioned. I explained that Carlos had sent me over and that I was looking for property for Jack Bellin.

Brando and I fell into easy banter right away. He had the ability to make a person feel very comfortable quickly, as if one had been his friend for a long time. He told me that he was home alone because Tarita was away for a few days, and that their son Teihotu was being looked after by Agnes. We talked about available land, and how difficult it was to acquire property in Tahiti, particularly for foreigners. Marlon explained that he himself had bought an island called Tetiaroa, and that it had not been easy to get permission from the local government to do so. Only a trip to Paris, over the local governor's head and somewhat against his wishes, had finalized the sale. When I explained that I had actually been to Tetiaroa in December and described my escapades on the reef, he absolutely roared with laughter. "If you survived that reef, you can survive anything," he mumbled in his gravely voice.

To this day, I honestly don't know if my crossing the reef at Tetiaroa had been a test that Marlon had cunningly devised for me, or if our meeting that day at his house in Punaauia was pure coincidence. Later on, in talking to his friends, I discovered that Marlon had a well-known reputation for "testing" people. This only confirms my suspicion that Jack may have told him about my interest in environmental design and that Marlon set me up just to see if I was tough enough to handle the challenges Tetiaroa would offer. In fact, Jack had been to my office before my first trip to Tahiti and borrowed a model I had made of a prototype lodge for a client who wanted a pre-cut, site-assembled building made of on-site lumber. The lodge was to sit lightly on the land, and be environmentally benign and adaptable to any location. The project never came to fruition, but the model had been sitting in my office when Jack stopped by. At the time, I didn't think of asking Jack who he wanted to show it to. It's quite possible that he showed it to Marlon.

Brando's house was right on the beach, one of the nicest beaches on the island of Tahiti. He told me that there was a hole in the reef, beyond the lagoon, that you could look through and see huge fish in the ocean beyond. He wanted to show it to me. He took off his *pareu* and bent over, searching for masks and fins in a bin. I must admit that I felt slightly awkward seeing his bare bottom and associated appendages within the first thirty minutes of our initial meeting. "We don't need bathing suits; let's go," he said. I felt a little uncomfortable, but figured "what the hell," and soon, I too was naked as a jaybird, following him out to the beach. He swam well and fast, and I had a tough time keeping up with him. I caught up just as he was motioning me to follow him into the hole in the reef. He was right. You could see a variety of great big ocean fish right there in front of you. It was like looking into an aquarium while being submerged in it. All of a sudden, in my peripheral vision, I spotted a large object practically next to me. "Oh my God, it's a shark!" Knowing that I was in a lagoon, not the ocean, I realized it may have been a lagoon shark and probably not dangerous, but I wasn't taking any chances, so I swam away as fast as I could. When I stopped for breath, Marlon, who had tailed me, was laughing so hard that he lost his snorkel. "You crazy bastard!" he said, "You really think you could out-swim a fucking shark?"

In the kitchen afterward, I remember sitting across from him at a small table. He had brought out two beers, a baguette, and a hunk of cheese, which he put in the middle between us. Marlon cut off a piece of cheese, cut it in half, ate one half, and left one half for me. I cut that one in half, ate one half, and left the other half for him. This continued until we were both eating tiny bits of cheese. The idea was to see who could leave the smallest slice for the other. We didn't speak. He obviously enjoyed playing games with people. I found it entertaining and willingly went along with it. I actually believe we got to know each other quite well that way. He was learning if I would follow him, and I was discovering how far he would go with his silly games. In a weird way we were establishing a bond. Out of the blue, after this curious lunch, Marlon suggested, "Why don't you stay here? There's plenty of room. I'll lend you my car so you can go get your stuff at the hotel." How could I possibly refuse?

That day marked the beginning of a wonderful friendship. It was February 20, 1970, my first day back in French Polynesia and the beginning of an adventure that would shape the rest of my life. When I returned from the hotel later in the day, and walked in with my bags, Marlon showed me my room and played the perfect host. He was charming and attentive, making certain that I was comfortable. He even had clean towels in my bathroom. Later we relaxed drinking rum punches while looking at the sunset. When I told him that I had done Summer Stock Theater one year with the famous aging German director, Erwin Piscator, he froze for an instant, reacting in a way that told me that I was treading in dangerous waters. I learned then and there that acting and, therefore, Hollywood, were out of bounds. I sensed that our relationship, if there was to be one, would not be based on his being a renowned Hollywood actor and me a curious and admiring fan. I was quite certain that he did not want to talk about his career as an actor. I respected that and never brought it up unless he did first, which was not often. Much later he told me that he himself had done Summer Stock with Piscator, and had lost respect for him after catching him being serviced by a young actress who wanted a leading role in his next play.

The phone rang and Marlon announced that his *amie* Tarita had just given birth! In a flash we were off to the hospital. I didn't go inside with him, but after a while he came out and proudly proclaimed that he was the father of a girl. She would be named Cheyenne. We ate dinner that night on the Papeete quay at the *roulottes*, open vans with small counters and stools outside to sit on. Delicious Chinese food was prepared right in front of us. Marlon told me that one reason he liked Tahiti so much was that he could go anywhere without people paying any attention to him. He hated being recognized and fawned over, and he enjoyed the anonymity. He was annoyed by what he called "fans' misplaced adoration," and

Top
A view of Moorea from Marlon's beach on Tahiti.

Bottom
Marlon's house in Punaauia, Tahiti.

A typical scene along the beach in Marlon's neighborhood.

was downright antagonistic toward the press. He said he was unworthy of all the attention. In Tahiti he was left alone and content. I couldn't have felt more content myself.

Marlon and Carlos respected each other. They loved to speak of world affairs, women, and all the craziness involved in living in Tahiti. And their *amies*, Agnes and Tarita, had become best friends since they had worked together in 1962 as actresses in *Mutiny on the Bounty*. Marlon had met them both on the set. Tarita, a young Tahitian dancer from Bora Bora, captivated Brando with her youth, shyness, warmth, and great beauty. At his urging she became his leading lady. Marlon fell in love with her in real life as well. In part, it was because of Tarita that Marlon decided to live in French Polynesia and raise his beloved little boy Teihotu there. And when Marlon had to leave the country occasionally, it was Carlos who took care of Marlon's affairs, and it was Agnes who looked after Teihotu.

Agnes took me around Tahiti in Marlon's car to look at properties. Unfortunately, the site recommended by Jack turned out to have a gravely beach with gray sand, not what I thought would attract people to Tahiti. In fact, I found that half of Tahiti's shores have black sand and rocky beaches, or no beaches at all. Agnes thought I should look for land on Moorea, as it was known for its beautiful white sand beaches. I told her I had seen some for myself over the Christmas holiday.

The day after Agnes and I toured Tahiti, I took her advice and went to Moorea again. I stayed a few days at Chez Pauline, my new friend's little guesthouse surrounded by her garden and the *tikis*! I rode around in a rented Mini Moke, a small, open Australian car not much bigger than and very similar to a golf cart. It had no sides or doors, just a windshield and a canvas roof. It was a delightful way to see the island, open to the air and the sights, and just rugged enough for the rough coral road. In talking to Pauline, Agnes's relatives and the Bali Hai boys, I was able to locate several properties that were for sale or lease. The Bali Hai boys were particularly helpful in giving me insights into construction materials, their costs, and all that it takes to run a hotel in Polynesia. When I returned to Punaauia, Marlon was very interested in what I had been doing and quizzed me on how I went about analyzing each property. I noted things like views, proximity to roads and access, types of soil and vegetation, the quality of the sand on the beach, where the sun rose and set, the winds, availability of fresh water, electricity, sewage disposal, and the quality of surrounding environs, including neighborhoods.

Within two weeks, I had collected information on fifteen properties on Moorea. I narrowed the list down to two that had particularly beautiful views and beaches. One, on Opunohu Bay, consisted of almost 20 acres and could be bought for $35,000 cash, but it seemed too high a price for property with only 80 meters of beachfront. Things change quickly though. Today, 20 acres with beachfront property on Opunohu Bay would fetch several million! The other site, on Cooks Bay, was perfect, except for one fact: the owner, Madame Leeteg, the widow of an American artist who had become famous for painting

Tahitian nudes on black velvet, made it a condition of the sale that I marry her. She had married Monsieur Leeteg after World War II, and when he died in a grisly motorcycle accident, Madame re-married. Soon after, her second husband suffered a heart attack and died too. I didn't want to be her next victim, and besides, I was already married. I can only go so far for a potential client.

Time and money were running out. I remembered the beach Dora and I had visited on our tour around Moorea. The Christmas picnic was etched in my mind, as was the fabulous view of Tahiti in the distance. I had thought even then that this was a perfect site for a hotel. Our tour guide at the time had mentioned that the property belonged to the queen of Tahiti. That comment seemed peculiar even then; I did not realize that Tahiti had a queen. But then again, there were many things I didn't know about Tahiti, and so I didn't question it. Now, slightly worried about returning to Los Angeles empty-handed, I went back to the queen's beach, had a beer, and mulled over my predicament. There was no doubt, this was a spot as close to perfect as we'd ever get. But there were drawbacks as well. The thought struck me that the queen might be interested in joining us as a partner. We could call it the Queen's Inn, or some such thing. The question was, how to contact her? I went to the mayor's office in Afareaitu, next to Chez Pauline, and was able to find the particular parcel on a map. When I showed it to the mayor's secretary and inquired whether the queen still owned it, she looked at me in amazement. "What queen? That beach belongs to Temarii Teai! There is no queen of Tahiti anymore." Boy, did I feel foolish! But what a pleasant surprise it was to learn that I didn't have to deal with royalty, even though the regal project might have been a lot of fun.

It didn't take long to find Teai; everyone knows where everyone else is on Moorea. When I met him and told him my story, he said, "If that property belongs to the queen of Tahiti, then I must be the king. Get on your knees before me!" It turned out that his property was about 25 acres, and included 100 meters of beach. It certainly had the views, but the one road that circled the island divided the property close to the beach. I decided to worry about that later, and started negotiations with the not-so-regal king. Surprisingly, rather than sell, he agreed to lease his land, and we fixed a fair price of $4,000 per year, for a period of ten years, renewable for another twenty. I was certain that I had found exactly what I had been looking for.

The next step was to check whether there were restrictions on buying or leasing land for a hotel project. A law from 1933 proved to be a hurdle I needed to overcome. The law had originally been written to protect Tahitian land from being overrun by the Chinese. The French were farm owners, not farmhands, and the Tahitians didn't particularly like working on farms, either. The French government needed labor to foster the economy, and so they brought the Chinese to Tahiti expressly to work on their farms. The Chinese jumped at the chance, particularly those from the southern provinces of China, which, at the time, had suffered a great depression. Unfortunately it turned out that the Chinese didn't take to farming either. They saved their money and began buying land from the Tahitians. The Chinese could bargain for very low prices, because the Tahitians were unfamiliar with making commercial real estate deals. They had inherited their property from their ancestors and completely failed to realize the land's value. Once the Chinese owned land, they built stores, which earned them a lot of money, which in turn allowed them to purchase more Tahitian land.

The French easily recognized that Tahitians were being taken advantage of, and being good administrators, they instituted a law to protect them from the Chinese. Of course, the law gave the French a measure of control over the land as well. In 1970 the law was still in effect, and stated that the French governor had to approve all land sales, particularly those to non-Tahitians. This was one reason it had taken Marlon such a long time to buy Tetiaroa.

I went to the office of the Tahiti Tourist Development Board in Papeete, and met with Alec Ata, its director. Like most Tahitians, Alec was of mixed heritage, a *demi*, meaning "half" in French. In general, a person was thought of as a *demi* if that person had recent European parentage and had adopted European customs. Actually, most Tahitians have mixed blood. Tahitians with purely Polynesian ancestry can only be found on the remote outer islands. Tahitians from the major islands, on the other hand, have procreated with Europeans from the time the Europeans arrived. The British left traces of their lineage when they first arrived under Wallis in 1767. Only a year later the French added to the mix under Bougainville. And yet another year later the British returned with Captain Cook. With the advent of whaling in the South Pacific around 1790, Tahiti had become a destination for ships from all over the world. The tough, hardy seamen who hunted whales for their oil throughout the 18th and 19th centuries would retreat to islands like Tahiti in the winter. Missionaries and traders appeared in their wake. Polynesian culture did not impose sexual restraints such as those suffered by prudish Europeans. Sex to them was as natural as it was enjoyable. The lovely and uninhibited Polynesian women welcomed European sailors with open arms.

With few exceptions, the French population living in Papeete in the early 1970s were doctors, lawyers, administrators, and military personnel. Tahitian *demis* were an educated middle class who worked for the French government, for the airlines and hotels, and in businesses of their own. The French school system was very good, and as far as I could tell, all children went through elementary school and most through high school. Higher education was not available in Tahiti. People went to France or New Zealand for college and university. The Chinese, who sent their children to their own schools, formed the commercial class. They owned and ran most every store in town. "Native" Tahitians, by and large, were fishermen. There was a large tuna fishing fleet right in Papeete Harbor. Native Tahitians worked on the docks, in restaurants, in construction,

In Moorea, each village along the road has its own church.

I loved sitting outside a church window on a Sunday listening to the choral singing.

Top
Typical Moorea vista.

Bottom
Moorea sunset.

View of Tahiti from Moorea.

or as household help. Some did not work at all. In a culture of sharing, it was enough if one member of a family had a job. The whole family could get along quite well on one paycheck. If all else failed, there were fish in the lagoon, fruit in the gardens, and coconuts in the trees.

The Tahiti Tourist Development Board in Papeete served about 70,000 tourists every year. Alec was a bright, well-educated, and amusing character, and he was also an Anglophile. Clearly, that was an advantage for me. Alec knew the importance of public relations, and always arranged to have the winner of the annual Miss Tahiti contest work in the tourism office with him. He introduced me to Tiare Higgins, a former Miss Tahiti who eventually became a UTA airline stewardess. She became a friend and later, in her capacity as stewardess, a wonderfully fast courier. She carried mail to and from my office in Los Angeles overnight, saving me weeks of potential lag time. Alec and I got along well, which pleased me, especially as he was the first of many who could, or could not approve our hotel project. He said he knew the "queen's" property on Moorea, thought it would work well as a hotel site, and gave me a list of officials and documents I would need in order to get government approval.

I went back on Moorea to sign an option agreement with Teai. I took the opportunity to look up Tiger, our entertainment guru at the Club Med Moorea. I remembered from my previous visit that he was looking for a new job, and so I asked if he might be interested in running a hotel. He said that he would think about it, and since he was due to visit the States, we arranged to meet back in Los Angeles the following month to discuss the matter further.

It was raining lightly when I left Cooks Bay that evening, but it appeared that the weather would soon clear. Outside the pass in the reef, however, the wind from the north began to tear into us. Large waves smashed into the port side of the ferry, and the canvas awnings flapped wildly. We could see nothing but sea spray. When it suddenly became terribly dark, the Captain shot off a couple of flares, and the crew jumped overboard! I was utterly amazed and greatly concerned. The other passengers and I didn't know what to do. We rocked back and forth in the relentless gale. It seemed more and more dangerous as the storm raged. Suddenly, men appeared out of the night from the sea. We learned that the swells had pushed our boat onto the reef. The sailors who had gone overboard had tried to dislodge it, but to no avail. We were stuck. The flares alerted the nearby Bali Hai Hotel, and they sent out staff paddling through the storm in canoes to find us and bring us in. After many crossings in the wind and rain, we were all safely back on land. Thankfully, no one had been hurt or lost. The Bali Hai Hotel lobby was packed with wet people and their soaking belongings, but the bar was open to all. The Keke II, battered but still afloat, was towed off the reef the next day.

As it happened, Jean Shelsher, the painter we had met at Club Med over the Christmas holidays, was dining with her boyfriend at the Bali Hai that night. She saw me, took pity, and invited me to dinner and then to stay with them at the Gump house. In the morning, after the storm had finally passed, the sun shone brilliantly over Cook's Bay. Imagine my delight to be staying in the house on the hill overlooking Cook's Bay, the very house that I had admired so dearly on my first day in Polynesia two months earlier.

I returned to Marlon's in Punaauia the next day. Tarita had gone to her sister's house in town. I don't remember seeing much of her at that time. Teihotu, their eight-year-old son, was about the house but would often disappear for a few days, and beyond going to school, didn't seem to have a discernible pattern to his life. I began to learn a good deal about Tahitian family life at the Brando residence. For instance, I discovered that it was not unusual for children to sleep in any bed they happened to fall into — in any house in the neighborhood. Houses were quite open at the time. Occasionally, I made room for a child I didn't know in my own bed. I may never have seen him or her before, or, for that matter, thereafter. I called these kids "intermittent children." I often wondered which parent belonged to which child and only slowly learned that Tahitian kids are often unofficially adopted by an aunt or a close friend. Teihotu, for example, was unofficially adopted by Agnes.

Unofficial adoption is an ancient Polynesian tradition, and serves four main purposes: it fosters social cohesion, with an emphasis on the community rather than the family; it is economically prudent as it allows sharing limited food supplies and labor, especially among the elderly; it helps form bonds with communities on other islands; and it takes care of the children born into young couples with often unstable relationships. Their children were simply "given away" to a friend or relative. I marveled at all of this until I understood that in Tahiti, people really look out for one another. They tend to live in small communities in which everyone knows everyone else. The elders keep an eye on the younger kids and make sure they stay out of trouble. Parents inform other parents where their children are at any given time. That there was a great love of children was evident, as kids were always welcome in their neighbors' homes. Love for a child, any child, was obviously more important than parentage.

Houses, particularly in the districts outside Papeete, were usually left open and unlocked during the daytime, Marlon's home included. Children entered at will. Adults, however, would announce themselves from the garden before coming in. There was very little theft. If an item went missing, it was assumed it had simply been "borrowed." Someone, not necessarily the person who "borrowed" it, would bring it back. On one occasion, I left my wallet, loose change, and passport on the bedside during a trip to Tetiaroa. Nothing had been disturbed upon my return days later. Life in Tahiti seemed endearingly charmed.

Marlon was fascinated by my extensive research on each of the potential Moorea hotel sites. He would go through my architectural and engineering notes with considerable interest. He kept a close eye on everything an architect must investigate and research in preparation for any project. And he pored over my long lists of all that is necessary to make this specific project, a hotel, successful. He looked at my plans and sketches, my hotel marketing surveys, and reports on the history of tourism in Tahiti. Every night he would quiz me on the day's progress. I visited various government offices for permits and banks for loans. I had to check on the prices and availability of materials, familiarize myself with the Investment Code for foreigners, and research prices people were paying for rooms, meals, drinks, and services at similar hotels. I was putting together a lot of information.

The Investment Code was of particular interest to Marlon. Low interest loans and customs-free imports were made available by the government to those who wanted to build hotels. Sometimes I'd wake up in the middle of the night to find Marlon going through my papers. At times this would annoy me, but I let it go, hoping he'd rely on me in the future. Obviously he was thinking a lot about how to develop Tetiaroa.

My work gave me a chance to get to know my way around Papeete, its sidewalk cafés, restaurants, and shops. Except for the government buildings, the town was made up of one-and two-story wood structures on old, narrow streets that were lined with shade trees planted in the colonial days. Chinese stores with living quarters above, surrounded the central market place offering fresh fish, fruit, vegetables, and dried vanilla beans. The scents were wonderful. I loved stopping at Vaimas Sidewalk Café, which overlooked the myriad of activities at the harbor. At Vaimas I met people like Ripley Gooding, who could usually be found there having his morning coffee. He was an old-timer, large and gregarious, with a shocking mane of white hair, always ready to swap stories with anyone who would listen. Ripley had been the proprietor of Les Tropiques, an early bungalow-style beach hotel from the 1920s. Everyone who was anyone traveling to Tahiti had stayed there at least once. He owned an island, a *motu*, in the Raiatea lagoon, 200 miles northwest of Tahiti. He had put in an underwater pipeline from the main coast, and I was interested in how he had done it. "If you want to get anything done in Tahiti," he would say, "you have to do it yourself." It was from gentlemen like him that I learned a lot about living on the islands, the good as well as the bad. I became a regular at the Ping Pong bookstore, where you could buy old naval charts, as well as signed black-and-white prints by Tahiti's renowned photographer, Sylvain. I bought several great prints for very little money, and I wish that I had bought even more.

During my walks through Papeete, I would occasionally run into Bengt Danielsson, a tall, bald man with a long gray beard, who browsed Ping Pong as carefully as I did. He was an ethnologist from Sweden and had crossed the Pacific with fellow ethnologist and Norwegian author Thor Heyerdahl on the famous balsa wood raft Kon-tiki in 1947. Starting in Peru and ending in the Tuamotus in eastern Polynesia, the voyage was an attempt to verify that early settlers of what is now called Polynesia could have come from South America. The expedition did not confirm that they actually had come from the Americas, but it did prove that it was possible to have come this way. Today the dominant theory is that Polynesians came from the West, not the East.

Danielsson, not unlike many other South Seas adventurers, had ended up in Tahiti for good, living "in the country," outside Papeete proper, with his lovely French wife, Marie Therese. It was always a pleasure to chat with him.

In speaking to Danielsson, and later reading Thor Heyerdahl, I learned a lot about the sea. During their passage across the vast distances of the Pacific, they were surprised to find many oil slicks and garbage flotsam appearing out of nowhere, hundreds if not thousands of miles from land. They realized that the world's garbage did not disappear once dumped in the ocean. In fact, the world's oceans are a dump for the world's pollutants. Though the oceans are constantly replaced through evaporation and rain, only pure water evaporates. The rest stays there. Pollutants and man-made chemicals, particularly those that are not biodegradable, remain in the ocean and build up over time. They don't dissolve, get digested, or disappear. Most marine life, about 90%, including marine plankton, algae, and corals, live at the surface of the oceans, no more than 80 to 100 meters deep. This is where life-giving photosynthesis occurs. This is the level of the ocean that provides nourishment from the bottom of the food chain, right through large fish and whales. Unfortunately, this is also the level at which most pollutants, pesticides, insecticides, chemical fertilizers, and detergents float. Man-made chemical "cides," as well as non-biodegradable sewage and garbage, are a danger to marine life. Corals are particularly sensitive. If coral reefs are killed, or even damaged or otherwise negatively affected by pollutants, the interdependent ecological balance of the ocean is thrown off. This is particularly dangerous to an atoll, as the coral reef is its only protection. Today we know that if we want to protect our environment, we must limit and control these pollutants. We must make sure that they are not simply dumped into the sea from ships, or carried out there through rain and drainage.

But at the time, boy, this was all news to me, and certainly apropos.

Marlon and I went to bars at night — Quinn's, Lafayette, and Zizu Bar, among others — to "check out the cost of drinks." Quinn's, the most famous and notorious watering hole in the South Pacific, was a bamboo-faced bar/dance hall right on the waterfront of Papeete Harbor. This was no dark nightclub. The front was wide open to the sidewalk, with tables on one side and a long mahogany bar on the other. The bar extended to the back, where the most unusual, unpartitioned, coeducational bathroom in the world was located. It consisted of a tile-walled room, about as big as a two-car garage, with a steel grate 6 inches off the concrete floor upon which one relieved oneself. It was flushed out every morning with a fire hose. Quinn's was rough and raucous at night, but during the day it was the meeting place for anyone who wanted to go downtown to have a drink, catch up on local gossip, or do business. "I'll meet you at Quinn's," was something one regularly heard. At dusk things began to change. Eddy Lund's Tahitian band would arrive and loyal patrons would drink and dance to the South Seas version of the fox trot until nightfall. After that, native girls from the outer islands, sailors from ships in the harbor, and locals out for a good time would drift in as the music became louder and faster. Someone would always shout, *Tamure!* Then the drummers would take over and everyone would switch to the traditional Tahitian dance, which consisted of knee-knocking men and swivel-hipped women moving faster and faster until one woman would inevitably jump up on a table. As people laughed and clapped, she would untie her *pareu* from her shoulder and roll it down low over her hips dancing wildly, furiously in a blur of hips and breasts until she practically fell off the table, the music simultaneously coming to a crescendo. Things over at the Zizu Bar were a bit different. Zizu catered to the most beautiful transvestites I have ever seen. At least it seemed so after a few rums. And the Lafayette was a large dance hall popular with the young, where it was not unusual for women to get into fights over men — real fist fights with black eyes, bloody noses, and everything. Marlon and I did a lot of "research."

Although it was rare that Marlon spoke about making movies or acting, he did talk despairingly about Hollywood sometimes. On one occasion, he told me about *Burn!*, a picture he'd shot in Colombia in 1969. Marlon, an outspoken advocate of human rights, had gotten so mad at the movie's director, Gillo Pontecorvo, for treating the actors badly and the natives without pity that he walked off the set and took a plane to Florida. He found Pontecorvo "uncaring and cruel," particularly to the Indians who were working as extras. Marlon talked about endless and unnecessary retakes in the hot sun. He thought about quitting the film, but eventually he was convinced to go back. I could tell that he had been really worked up about it. He had wanted to work with Pontecorvo since he'd directed *Battle of Algiers*, a film that Marlon had much admired. He wanted to make a film that made a strong political statement, and the story of *Burn!* had to do with colonialism, slavery, and revolution. He played a British agent inciting rebellion among sugar plantation slaves in the Caribbean. It was a natural for Marlon. I suspect he was upset because he was disappointed that a man he respected professionally did not show consideration for those less fortunate than himself. In Marlon's eyes, the director himself embodied the colonial spirit the movie criticized.

Marlon was a rebel and revolutionary at heart. He had met and made friends with some true revolutionaries amongst the Black Panthers, the radical Black Power movement that was strong in the U.S. during the 1960s and early 1970s. He said he had talked revolutionary politics with several of them, and in particular about violence as a means to a political end. This was interesting to me, as I had also encountered Panthers at the Berkeley founding convention of the Peace and Freedom Party in 1967. The party platform was largely focused on the anti-war movement, but its members were also deeply committed to fighting oppression of both African Americans and Native Americans. The party reached its pinnacle during the Vietnam War, when they nominated candidates on both local and national levels. Personally, I had been turned off by the manifest anger of the Panthers. They seemed out of control and, in my view, not in sync with the philosophy of the Peace and Freedom Party, which was, after all, in support of peace. Anger and its violent expression went too far for me. Marlon had demonstrated against violence and the war alongside Martin Luther King, and agreed with me. Yet he also had great empathy for the Black Panthers and their frustrations. We talked about the futility of violence and revenge, about anger, and how much personal emotion had to be controlled to achieve social change. It was something he, as a self-admitted control freak, knew quite a bit about. Evidently, during *Burn!*, Marlon and Pontecorvo both lost control of themselves. As I was to discover over the years, mistrust and the ensuing need for control were rather characteristic of Marlon's persona. It was a side of Marlon that was sometimes hard to deal with.

While staying with Marlon in Punaauia those first weeks of our acquaintance, I had a chance to meet his friends. Some of them would become my friends too, and are to this day. I clearly recall the morning I met Manutea Knight. I heard someone calling Marlon's name at the front door. Marlon wasn't in, and so I went out to greet the guest, and there she was, a stunningly beautiful young lady in a bright red *pareu*, long brown hair hanging over her shoulders and a flowered *couronne* on her head. I was immediately enchanted. No, I was smitten. She said that Marlon was invited to dinner at her mother's that evening, and that I was welcome to come along. It turned out to be a most fortuitous dinner party, as Manutea and her family would play important roles in both my personal and professional life in Tahiti.

I'll never forget that evening. The setting was magical. Drinks were served on the lawn with the sun setting over Moorea across the sea. Inside a thatched hut on the beach, the dinner table was draped with a colorful *pareu*, and set with dishes made of large pearl shells, elegant silverware and candlesticks, as well as cut-crystal glassware. Tea's mother, Purea, had recently been widowed. She was, and still is, a true matriarch. She lived a life that was a perfect mix of Tahitian and European culture. Purea, a descendant of royal Tahitians, had married an American, John Reasin, in 1938. She had the good fortune of inheriting many Tahitian properties, and was able to raise her two children on a beach 19 km from Papeete. The kids, Manutea (Tea) and Tihony (Johnny), were home-schooled by their father. They learned to speak Tahitian from their playmates on the beach and from the help at home. Johnny now lives on one of the islands in the Gambier Archipelago, 1,000 miles southeast of Tahiti, where he has created for himself a life not unlike the one in which he was raised. In a remote part of the world, he built his own home for his Tahitian wife and two children, home-schooled the kids, and savored a life of resourcefulness and independence amid nature. Johnny and his family remain the sole inhabitants of the island.

As a young adult, Tea spent some time in Hawaii, where she met her future husband, an American, Gordon ("Zeke") Knight. They had moved to Tahiti to raise their three children. Zeke was the Assistant Manager of the Bank of Tahiti. He was from New England, preppy, a great sailor and athlete, with an easy-going, one-of-the-boys charm. He became a close friend and would also become a significant player in my greatest Tahitian adventures. When I met them in 1970, they were living on the beach in Punaauia, "out in the country," just down the street from Marlon's. Unlike Marlon's house, which was fronted by a sea wall, their beachfront home included the best little pocket of white sand around. Their lawn led straight down to the beach. It was a truly idyllic setting, complete with a well-manicured coconut grove, large thatched rooms open to the breezes, an outdoor kitchen and eating area amid flowering gardens, and a whale of a view of the sunset and the sea. What a wonderful way to raise kids! Zeke, Tea, and Purea were close to Marlon. Right from the start of my time in Tahiti, they took me under their wing, cared for me as a close friend, and became some of my dearest friends ever. Their house has been always open to me and I consider them my Tahitian "family."

I cannot say enough about the truly caring and communal nature of the lifestyle in Tahiti. It is so far removed from the competitiveness we know in the United States and the rest of the Western world. It draws you in and seduces you immediately. I remember waking up before dawn to the chorus of roosters, and walking home late on dark, unlit roadways. It almost seemed as if civilization had not quite made it there yet, and I didn't miss it. There were almost no cars or other accoutrements defining "class." Tahiti had a paved road around the island, but the population outside Papeete lived very much like those on Moorea. Little houses were strung out along the circular road forming communities within walking distance of Chinese stores, schools, and churches. Everyone in each community knew each other. There were, of course, some people less fortunate than others. But the "poor" were not in the state of poverty one encounters in other parts of the world. There were no shantytowns or beggars in the streets of Papeete. The French had introduced a system of education, healthcare, welfare, and infrastructure that provided for the basic needs of all members of its society. As far as I could understand, status in the community was based on interpersonal relationships, talents, and personal achievement, rather than on family background or accumulated material goods. Properties were handed down from generation to generation, and had not been subdivided yet. There, the more affluent and the not so fortunate *popaas* lived side by side with the *demis*, Chinese, and Tahitians; as in any community, not everyone was a close friend, but people knew each other and were conscious of their neighbors. People looked after each other's kids, and, as was the custom, welcomed them in each other's homes regardless of status or background. I remember a day when Dora, Sabrina, and I arrived from Los Angeles at Marlon's house in Punaauia. I watched Sabrina run across the beach and into the water, whereupon a burly Tahitian man quickly and gently scooped her up and back onto the sand. He turned out to be the taxi driver who had delivered us there from the airport earlier that morning. He was one of Marlon's good neighbors, who had recognized Sabrina as a child unfamiliar with the coral heads in the lagoon. One of Marlon's other neighbors owned Quinn's, the notorious waterfront bar.

Families lived in traditional, open thatched-roof houses, which were distinguished by separate buildings for each "room" in a house. Zeke, Tea, and her mother lived in such a house. The newer low-roof houses with wood or masonry walls have all their rooms under one roof. This is how Marlon's house was constructed. There were also a few charming old colonial houses with tin roofs from the 1800s, but they were starting to disappear. Thatch roofs could be more expensive than tile or even corrugated metal roofs, if you had to buy labor and materials. But the Tahitians without ready cash were very adept at weaving their own roofing materials. The newer concrete block houses with metal roofs, though "modern," were a lot hotter and more uncomfortable to live in than the traditional thatched-roof homes with woven bamboo walls. I was very drawn to a lifestyle that allowed for living out in the open under thatched-roofs, amid fruit trees and flowering, well-tended gardens. However, I was not blind to the fact that it took a lot of money to live this way if you also wanted to have the modern conveniences like electricity, hot water, washing machines, cars, and telephones. But if you could do without them, the benign climate and a supportive society would allow you to live well for very little money. I was happy to have found a place where rich and poor could partake in the beauty of nature side by side.

The women of Polynesia have always been somewhat of an enigma to me. They are at once open and reserved, exotic and mysterious. They smile and laugh easily, but rarely converse, except amongst themselves. When Tarita and her friends would chat in the kitchen, Marlon was always sure that "they're talking about us, Bernie." Tarita would rarely sit with us while we had dinner. She preferred eating by herself or with a friend in the kitchen. Marlon would occasionally insist that she eat with us, but she never felt comfortable taking part in our conversations. This, I was told, was quite typical, for in traditional Tahitian homes, the women often eat separately from the men or at one end of the table where they can talk among themselves. Perhaps this is because some men love to eat *fafaru*, a dish of putrid fish, which, though delicious, has a horrible odor. Early accounts written by missionaries refer to a social taboo having to do with men and women eating together. This taboo, I am told, had to do with an ancient superstition about men who ate in the presence of women going blind. Be that as it may, dining was one of the rare instances when women and men did not share the same social status. Other than that, traditional Tahitian society did not seem to distinguish status based on gender. In fact, the ancient Tahitian language did not include a distinguishing pronoun for "he" or "she." While there seemed to be a division of work inside the home, it was not rigid and did not seem to carry any social judgment. The women did most of the housework and cooking, but some women worked outside while their men took care of things at home, including watching the children and cooking. On really festive occasions, the men often built an earth oven for cooking bananas, breadfruit, and pig, as well as the fish they had caught. Generally, I was struck by the equality between men and women, but I also noticed that the fishermen in the tuna fleet were all men, and that it was the women who sold the fish in the market. The fact that Tarita, Agnes, and their friends preferred to eat separately seemed to be based on the curious Tahitian custom from pre-Westernized days, and not a symbol of the lower status of women in the household. In fact, in many ways women in Tahiti seemed more influential than men. They made both familial and community decisions, and were active in the political arena.

On the rare occasion that Tarita joined us at the table, I learned that a lot could be communicated without speech. She might look at me or at Marlon and signal "please pass the salt" or "may I have some bread" by raising her eyebrows slightly and pointing with her nose toward the salt or bread. Her movement was so subtle that it was not even noticeable unless you were trained to perceive it. Only after a gesture had been repeated several times, with perhaps a forward motion of the chin towards the object desired, did it become clear to me what she was asking for. Much is still "said" by both men and women using this language of the eyes: "It's over there in the next room" (eyes to the side and a slight tilt of the head in the direction of the other room); "Don't you dare mention his name" (eyes suddenly wide open for a millisecond); "yes" (just raised eyebrows, no raised nose); or "no" (no movement of the eyebrows, just a slight downward motion of the chin and lower lip). It took me a while to get used to this. At first I missed a lot as the only speaking person amongst a group of Tahitians, but gradually I learned to "speak" silently like they do.

Tahitians read body language like no others. It is said that they know more about you before you open your mouth than you know about yourself. Marlon, either a quick study or more instinctive than most Westerners, was readily adept at reading body language. This facility served him well on stage. His antennas were alert, not only in reading people, but also in communicating silently to transmit fear, anger, power, or pathos equally well.

The European habit of greeting each other with a kiss on both cheeks is a custom in Polynesia as well. This leads to a certain immediate sense of closeness even between strangers. Tahitians use *tu* instead of the more formal *vous* as is required in France, which reinforces the feeling of familiarity. Both create instant intimacy. To me these practices seemed warm and accepting, and delightfully feminine from women. The women in Tahiti are naturally conscious of their femininity: the way they dress, the way they walk, and their mannerisms exude a natural beauty. I have always enjoyed going to Polynesian Sunday church services (I love listening to the choral singing!), where the women dress up in long, white, high-collared colonial dresses and white straw hats. Even the largest of these women, and there are many, I find very beautiful. There is no doubt that many Tahitian women are gifted athletes, excelling in fishing and paddling, but it seems to me that they are also proud of their femininity and enjoy showing it.

Femininity is a special value in Tahiti. So much so that Tahitian boys are sometimes brought up as "girls." Initially, it was a surprise for me to learn that it's perfectly all right with everyone to raise a young boy as a "girl" if he exhibits particularly feminine characteristics and prefers to be considered as a girl. These males, who are called *mahu*, often grow up doing what is elsewhere traditionally identified as "woman's work," such as cooking and housework, or waitressing, none of which is considered at all demeaning. *Mahus* are accepted and valued as good and sociable employees, particularly in the hotel and restaurant businesses. I have yet to see any signs of discrimination against them.

Tahitian women are feminine in spite of their large feet! Polynesians are apt to have larger feet than Europeans or Americans because they walk barefoot. Before the Europeans arrived, there were no shoes. Period. In the 1960s, a French friend of Tea's, Gilbert Letty, opened a women's shoe store, Bata, in Papeete and made a fortune selling shoes to women who didn't even wear them! Because they are barefoot all the time, they develop unique ways of using their feet, such as picking up things with their toes. But the corker for me was when Alice walked in on Tarita one day, and found her cleaning the toilet with one of her feet!

Marlon liked to tell the story of his trying to buy a pair of high heels for Tarita in Beverly Hills, during the time they were dubbing *Mutiny on the Bounty*. After Tarita had tried on several pairs, all of which were too tight, he said to the salesperson: "Just give me the boxes; she can wear those."

Top
Typical corrugated metal roof house.

Right
Typical thatched-roof house.

Top
Zeke and Tea's house.

Bottom
Purea's house.

Tumata walking in the garden at her father's house.

April 1970

THE TAHITI SAFARI CLUB

Living with Marlon
Dancing Girls

I returned to Los Angeles with an enormous amount of investigative real estate research in my suitcase. Jack, of course, was eager to see what I had found out. I brought back option papers for two properties, both conditioned on French government approvals. We only had eight days to exercise the options: either to buy the Marchal property or to lease the Teai property. I had taken photographs, brought back maps, and made sketches of both. Jack found the Marchal property at Opunohu Bay less attractive and too expensive, but he liked the Teai property. He shared my concern that the road was too close to the beach. It was only 20 meters from the water, and there was barely enough space for the main building of a hotel and a dock. The rooms would have to be on the mountain side of the road, which, fortunately, was quite flat for a couple of hundred meters until the mountain started its steep ascent. It would be a problem for the guests to cross the road. I did some more sketches and was able to convince him that if the neighbors and the government agreed to move the road, all problems would be solved. Moving the road would increase the value of the neighboring lands, and so I had high hopes that both the neighbors and the government would agree. Jack would have to take a chance. And I was sure he would, because the Teai site offered one more advantage: the Moorea airport was only a five-minute drive away. The small airport had been built recently and was used for flights to and from Tahiti. By air, Tahiti was only ten minutes away. Air Tahiti flew Norman Britain Islanders, nine-passenger planes that were operated like an inter-island taxi service. Obviously, it would be convenient for our hotel guests to be so close to the airport.

Shortly after my return, Tiger arrived in Los Angeles and, as promised, I introduced him to Jack. An avid scuba diver, Tiger wanted to join us in the project, and make the hotel a destination for divers. Jack and I liked the idea, and Tiger, with his experience working in a management position at a resort in Moorea, seemed like a perfect fit. As a Frenchman, he would be able to cope with the authorities and their rules and regulations concerning the hotel business. Tiger agreed that the Teai property, which he knew quite well, had great promise in spite of the road problem. Jack decided to exercise the option on our word, without ever having been to Moorea, much less having seen the property. It was a leap of faith and he took it. We were happy to be in business together, and we decided to call the hotel The Tahiti Safari Club, inspired by hotel designs I had admired in Kenya several years earlier.

I contacted Teai by telegram and told him that a check to seal the option was in the mail, and that I would be back within a month. Jack was too busy to fly to Tahiti himself, and so it was up to me to finalize the deal. He wired money for the option to the owner, and we celebrated the beginning of our joint project in the South Pacific. Now it was time for me to draw more detailed plans and prepare financial statements for the Tahitian government and the banks. Jack's job was to raise money. It didn't take long for him to find our first investors. Two of his friends, airline pilots, joined us, and Jack drew up a deal between them, Tiger, and me. We would all become partners in the Tahiti Safari Club, the proceeds of which would be divided in accordance with each individual's investment in the project. Jack and his two friends would put up the seed money. The government would help with a bank loan. I would put up my time in preparing plans and getting permits, and Tiger would become the manager. Jack, Tiger, and I would share supervising construction.

I started drawing architectural plans. Tiger set himself up in my office and worked on the budget, financial statements, and all the other paperwork we needed to get government approval and bank loans. Within a month or so, I was ready to go back to Tahiti to present our plans.

Marlon welcomed me back and insisted that I stay with him. He told me that Dora and

Sabrina could visit anytime, and that Sabrina and Teihotu would be great playmates. Marlon was really interested in my drawings and budgets for the hotel. I set about making the rounds at the various offices that had to approve the project so that we could take advantage of the Investment Code incentives. That was something Marlon was particularly interested in: the French Territorial government allowed a great many benefits for the construction of new hotels. I don't think I quite realized it then, but Marlon was mulling over construction plans of his own.

Marlon and I spent wonderful evenings with Carlos that spring. I now regret not having had a chance to visit with Carlos more often. He lived a fascinating and unusual life, and was a great raconteur, but shortly after my stay with Marlon that spring, Carlos passed away. The dead were buried right away, as is the custom throughout the tropics, because they don't use embalming methods and the heat takes its toll on a decaying body. Marlon, who was in Paris at the time, got word of Carlos' death, hopped on a plane that very night, and was back in Papeete the next morning. The funeral was to be a State affair due to Carlos' consular rank.

Carlos was large in stature but small in frame. As Marlon told the story of Carlos' funeral, the coffin maker didn't build the coffin for poor Carlos' body, but for his stature. When the gravediggers tried to put the coffin in the ground at the Papeete cemetery, they discovered that they had dug a hole in the right size for the body, but too small for the coffin. As Marlon described it, the invited guests looked stunned and didn't move for a while, but as the sun beat down relentlessly, slowly the crowd — the men in their best black suits, and the women in their long white dresses and white hats — retreated under the trees and waited for someone to dig a larger hole. That took some time, because they had to find shovels first. At one point, everyone who had moved into the shade started gossiping and seemed to temporarily forget why they were there in the first place. At the gravesite, Marlon, who had dressed for the occasion, was sweating profusely under his straw hat and suit, and couldn't suppress laughing at the situation. It was so typically Tahitian. He said he took off his hat to cover his face and hide his giggling. It must have looked like he was crying, standing there in the sun by the empty hole with the casket protruding into the air. Carlos would have loved it.

I went back to Tahiti several times that year and was able to get the required approvals, as well as permission to move the road further away from the beach. Dora and Sabrina came with me whenever they could. We all stayed at Marlon's, and after a while his house felt like our home away from home. When we got the final go-ahead for the hotel from the government, Jack arrived. It turned out that there was no money to move the road, and therefore, no space to build the main hotel building. So we started building a couple of bungalows along the beach, which, after a while, caught the public's attention. One fine day, a Tahitian approached Jack on the site and asked, "Who are you, and what are you building on my land?" It was not long before forty-five people, all related to Teai, were coming out of the bushes, insisting that each had a claim to the property. It was a real shock for Jack, and he became furious at the whole situation. The forty-five claims proved a major embarrassment for the government, who had approved our project; the Notary, who had approved the title; Alec Ata, who was in fact a relative of Teai, and should have known better; and, of course, for me, who had arranged the whole affair in the first place. The problem was that in Tahiti, extended families do have the right to claim ownership of what was once communal land, and apparently they don't hesitate to come out of the woodwork to do so. It remains a real problem for any outsider trying to purchase land there, and it was terribly frustrating for all of us. It took a full year to resolve the situation, but eventually Jack bought the property from the Teai family for $60,000.

All this finagling took so much time that Tiger had to find another job and eventually left Tahiti for a while. I was as helpful as I could be, and really wanted the project to work out, but at a certain point, Jack decided to move ahead on his own. In the end, Jack was able to construct a much smaller version of the hotel than we had planned. Four years later, in 1974, Hollywood Jack, as he was called, sold it for a reputed $450,000. He left Tahiti soon thereafter and I haven't seen him since, but I'm eternally grateful to him for introducing me to Tetiaroa and Marlon Brando. The Tahiti Safari Club has subsequently been sold, re-sold, re-sold yet again, and enlarged. The road was eventually moved back away from the beach as I had originally suggested, greatly expanding the property along the beach. The hotel has been renamed and is now called the Sofitel Iaora. It is one of the premier hotels on Moorea.

During the time I was working on the Tahiti Safari Club throughout 1970 and early 1971, I was living with Marlon and Tarita in Punaauia, spending about a week each month at their house. A bedroom was always ready for me when I arrived. Whether Marlon was there or not, I was always welcome. On one occasion, Marlon picked me up at my house in L.A. and sent me off from LAX with a note to Tarita saying "Bernard est avec nous." I had become part of the family.

Marlon and I often talked about Tetiaroa. Not only what could be done there, but also what should be done there. Did he have a responsibility to the Polynesian people as owner of the thirteen *motus* in the lagoon? He owned the islands, but the lagoon and reefs belonged to the people, and what he did on the land would inevitably affect the lagoon and the reefs. The ecology of both are so intertwined that it is difficult to define exactly where the specific environmental responsibilities of the owner begin and end. Marlon also wanted to be respectful of Tetiaroa's history. Before contact, it had been a place where Tahiti's nobility

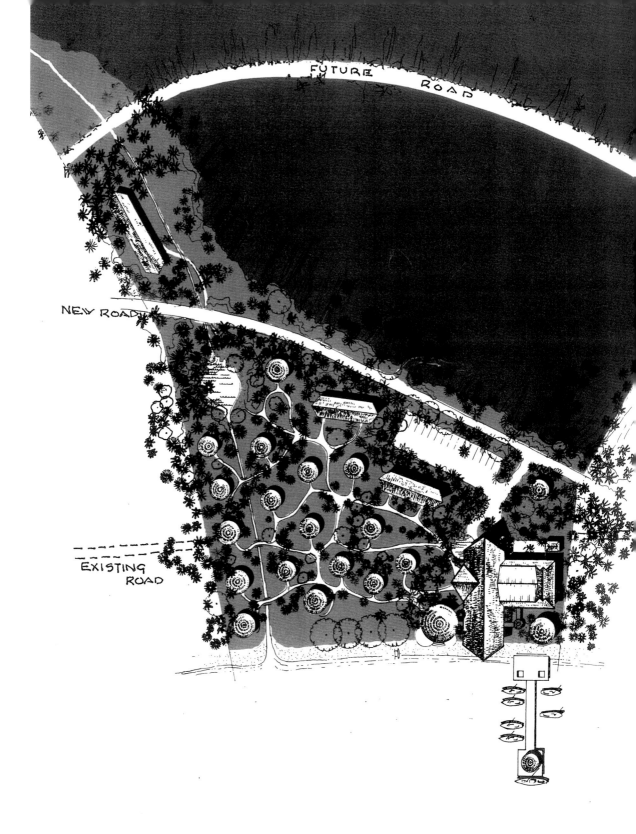

FUTURE ROAD

NEW ROAD

EXISTING
ROAD

First plan for the Tahiti Safari Club.

Top
A sketch for the TSC.

Bottom
Beginning to build the TSC, 1970.

would go to "vacation." It is said that they would fatten up on the plentiful fish and coconuts, and lie under the trees planted there expressly to provide shade for them; this would help them "bleach" their skin, the royal sign of both health and wealth. Marlon had been informed that there were archaeological sites on some of the *motus*. He wanted to locate them and insisted that the sites be preserved should he ever develop the land.

Marlon learned about Tetiaroa and its history from friends like Paul Faugerat, who was descended from an old, aristocratic Tahitian family. Paul was in his mid-fifties, a tall, imposing man, muscular and attractive with a wide, engaging smile and a full head of dark hair, graying only at the temples. His strong grip was that of a man who had worked with his hands all his life, a happy man with a cocky wit. His family had large land holdings, and when I met him he had become one of the last owners of a great copra plantation on the outskirts of Papeete. He was financially comfortable, as he had sold some property in 1962 which would later become the site of the first modern hotel in Tahiti, the Maeva Beach Hotel. Paul still worked on the plantation every day alongside his workers. He was producing 120 tons of copra a year. Mommy Purea, who had known him since childhood, said he was known as *le coq de la cour* in school, which translates poorly as "the rooster in the hen house." Handsome and a good dancer, he was much sought after by the ladies. When I met him, he was wooing a young, beautiful German lass named Jenny, who eventually became his wife and the mother of their three children. An enterprising man, he built the first drive-in movie theatre in Tahiti at a time when there were not even a lot of cars on the island. That situation was soon to change, and the theatre became a great success. Later, in the 1980s, Paul donated a part of his land to the government on which to build the first university in Tahiti.

Paul and Marlon were good friends and had gone to Tetiaroa together many times by the time I entered the picture. It was he who told Marlon about the old days, and the schooners that would arrive from Tetiaroa, their holds filled with fresh copra, emitting pungent aromas of coconut oil that would permeate the whole of Papeete Harbor. He spoke of the *tupaupa'us*, "ghosts" who would drive sailors crazy, and *maraes*, sacred religious structures from pre-contact days. He knew how to build with coconut wood, which trees were male or female, which were too young or too old to be used, and which gave the best leaves for weaving *niau*, the thatched roofing material. He told me, "Bernard, you are sitting in a lumber yard, and you don't even know it," and explained that a coconut trunk could not only be used as a post, but could be made into planks. But the trunk, unlike other trees, has the sap in the center; therefore the center is soft and is useless as lumber. It's the outer edges near the bark that are strong. That is why the trees can withstand high winds. The wood is so dense that hardened steel nails must be used rather than common nails. He explained that before nails were introduced to the islands, lashings of braided coconut fiber (*nape*) were used as fasteners. Paul also made me understand the importance of working side by side with Tahitians on construction projects. He said that one couldn't just give them the plans and leave. It had to be a collaborative effort. Paul was a fount of information, but he really spooked Marlon with his ghost stories. Marlon refused to listen to them. "Paul, a coconut must have fallen on your head," he'd say. As a matter of fact, though, Paul Faugerat is one of the few people in Tahiti who actually had a coconut drop on his head and survived to tell the tale! Perhaps that explains his cocky smile.

Throughout 1970, Marlon and I had visited an influential American ex-patriot named William Robinson (Roby) on several occasions. He was one of a handful of fascinating, colorful characters living in Tahiti. He had circumnavigated the globe in his 32-foot ketch, Svaap, the smallest boat ever to do it, and had written a bestseller about the voyage called *10,000 Leagues Over the Sea*. After discovering Tahiti on that trip, he returned and stayed. He lived on the beach in a commodious Tahitian thatched-roof house with his young Chinese-Thai *amie* and three beautiful daughters. If I remember correctly, his was the only property along the road "in the country" that was walled and gated.

Roby played a major part in the eradication of filariasis, a mosquito-borne disease that had been endemic in Tahiti. He also founded an elephantiasis clinic on the island that proved instrumental in controlling that dreadful disease. He owned a Polynesian atoll in the Tuamotu Archipelago, and Marlon and I would quiz him about it, trying to discover as much as we could about atolls. Roby told us about the Ghyben-Herzberg fresh water lens, which is the layer of rainwater floating on top of seawater that permeates the soil or coral base of an atoll. Since fresh water is lighter than salt water, it floats on the surface, very much like oil does on water. Roby told us that Tahitians use dogs to find fresh water, as they are able to smell the fresh water lens located a few inches below the sand. They dig a little and lap it up.

Roby's daughters, Hina, Tumata, and Rampa, had become the most famous teenaged dancers in Tahiti. They performed at local hotels and in competitions. Roby would stand in the background, tall, thin and elegantly dressed in white, while the girls performed exotic traditional Tahitian dances. These dances were sometimes slow and beautifully lyrical, at other times openly erotic. I recall the finale of one dance in particular. Tumata and a young man were dancing on top of a large drum. Both dressed in short *pareus*, they danced leisurely at first, eyeing each other carefully. Their hips swayed in an exaggerated oscillation to the slow cadence of a deep drum beat. Tumata's long, shiny black hair spilled across her bare shoulders with every motion. As the rhythm got faster and faster, the two dancers threw caution to the wind. Facing each other, hips and legs gyrating in a blur, it became a contest between them. Who could dance the fastest and the longest? Just when it seemed that they could go on no longer, the young man jumped off, the drum beat stopped, and Tumata, hidden behind her cascading hair, knelt down and then slowly, gracefully descended from her drum. It was quite a show and the audience loved it. Roby would hustle the girls off as soon as the performances were over to "protect" them from potential suitors. There was always a buzz around town about this handsome old yachtsman and philanthropist, his beautiful native "wife," and his three lovely, well-guarded daughters who all lived behind stone walls on gated property.

As an adult, Tumata became a leader in the country's arts and crafts movement, as well as its most cherished traditional dancer. She founded her own dance school and dance company. Together with a talented Tahitian choreographer, she started Les Grandes Ballet de Tahiti. They have become instrumental, and quite controversial, in combining Tahiti's traditional dances with modern dance expressions, an evolution that does not always sit well with traditionalists. She and I have stayed friends, and in 2001, I arranged for her company to perform at the Hollywood Bowl. It was greeted as a critical success.

Both the friendships and professional relationships I developed through Marlon in those early years in Tahiti were important to me on many levels. I was making life-long friends, and I felt that I was becoming a part of Tahitian society as I learned more and more about local customs and business practices. Due to many of these relationships, opportunities opened up for me in the South Pacific, both in environmental planning and architectural work. Years later, I would design several residences and hotels, and even a shopping center.

It was around September 1970, that Marlon first began openly expressing interest in developing ideas for Tetiaroa's future, and officially asked for my help. He had owned the atoll since 1966, and had been there many times with family and friends on short camping trips. He was absolutely enthralled with the beauty and serenity of the place, and wanted others to enjoy it too. There was, of course, no electricity, housing, running water, or toilets on the atoll, and, as I had experienced firsthand, there was no easy access across the reef. A whale boat had once capsized attempting to go over the reef and, unfortunately, one person lost his life. But access or not, Marlon had dreams that he now wanted to realize.

He told me that he envisioned opening the atoll to artists and intellectuals. He wanted to invite friends of his, like the writers James Baldwin and Tennessee Williams. He toyed with the idea of allowing his friends Dick Gregory and Russell Means from the Black Civil Rights and the American Indian movements to establish a retreat there. He even talked to Hugh Hefner about a resort. Marlon had a talented Hollywood art director, Mac Johnson, make some wonderful watercolor sketches. He wanted a first-class establishment. Marlon's ideas ran from the silly to the sublime, from the possible to the ludicrous, but they were all sincere. He had thought about importing elephants to do heavy physical work, and of making Tetiaroa a community dedicated to world peace, with the Maharishi Mahesh Yogi at its helm. Above all, Marlon wanted to keep the atoll free from pollution. He was adamant about it. He had contacted the Cousteau Society and scientists the world over. He had talked to hotel developers, and to Alec Ata regarding Tahiti tourism, but none of his development ideas had ever coalesced until I came on board.

We talked and talked and talked, sitting on the beach under the stars. We explored questions that weighed heavily on our minds. If one owns an island in the middle of nowhere, does one have the right to change it, to "develop" it? If so, why — just because one "owns" it? Where does this right come from? The concept of land ownership is not universal. Nomads in the Sahara, in Australia, and in the Arctic do not subscribe to ownership of land. For that matter, the early Tahitians, before contact with Europeans, did not understand the concept of individual ownership either. They "owned" land communally. In communist, as well as capitalist countries, the government owns land, they say, for the "greater good of the population." Historically, if land had natural resources — water or minerals, for instance — societies fought over control and the winner then "owned" the water or minerals. That's ownership by the right of conquest. And do we have the right to destroy what we own? Does one have a duty to society, or to the environment? Marlon was adamantly against pollution and for environmental protection, long before either was popular. He had made a promise. He said, "I am the atoll's guardian. I promised the former owners I would keep and preserve it for the Tahitians." He wanted to continue to enjoy and appreciate the atoll as it was. On the other hand, he wanted others to enjoy it too. Would the mere presence of others change it? These were good questions, and we needed to explore practical answers.

I was able to convince him that what he needed was a Master Plan for the atoll, a program that would meet his lofty dreams and make economic, engineering, and environmental sense. Tetiaroa seemed like a perfect laboratory for enlightened and sustainable development. Marlon considered my views carefully, and in early 1971, he asked me to author a Master Plan for Tetiaroa Atoll.

Photo by JF

Photo by PF

Top
Marlon, his sister Jocelyn, Alice, Tea, and Paul Faugerat.

Bottom
Marlon and Jenny Faugerat.

PLANNING PARADISE

Setting the Island on Fire
In Brando's Bedroom

Marlon and I had spent several months in discussion before he and I signed a contract in October, 1971. I quickly put together a small research team consisting of my Los Angeles associate Ron Smart, and architects and engineers I had worked with back in the States. We were able to use information Marlon had previously gathered from several scientists. One, Carl Hodges, had been experimenting with growing vegetables using a minimum of irrigation (nutriculture), and with raising fish (aquaculture) in the States, as well as in Abu Dhabi in the Arabian Peninsula. His findings would be critical to us, as we knew that atolls had very little fresh water. Another specialist lent his ecological expertise on atoll environments. Economic statistics were available from a company that had conducted a major study on tourism in Tahiti for the Tahitian government just a few years before. All of these experts had particular knowledge about the unusual environmental and social conditions of French Polynesia, and all were eager to participate.

I learned from Marlon that Tetiaroa is an atoll composed of thirteen islets, or *motus*, that lie 32 miles north of the island of Tahiti. The *motus* are surrounded completely by a fringing reef about 4 or 5 miles in diameter, unbroken by passes. The most recent inhabitant had been a Mrs. Duran, the daughter of a Canadian dentist, Dr. Williams, who had been given the atoll by King Pomare in appreciation for dental services rendered to the King's child. King Pomare was the last of the Pomare Dynasty, who ruled Tahiti until 1891. After retiring, Dr. Williams ran a coconut plantation on Tetiaroa for many years. After his death in 1937, Mrs. Duran lived on the atoll until it was sold to Marlon by her daughter in 1966. Mrs. Duran was a kind but eccentric woman, a recluse who collected stray dogs and cats in Tahiti and brought them to the atoll by boat. Apparently, Mrs. Duran was blind in the end and lived on one of the *motus* with a Chinese-Tahitian family and a couple of copra workers. She told Marlon that she got around the islet holding onto a rag wrapped around a wire that had been carefully tied to certain *tamanu* trees in order to guide her from place to place. Several visitors had written about Tetiaroa, including Somerset Maugham, who mentioned that the island's dogs had eaten all the cats that had been brought in to eat the rats, and therefore had to learn to fish for themselves. I learned that a leper had lived on the atoll at one time, and the remains of his house were still there. There was a small graveyard where Dr. Williams, his wife, and sister were buried, along with a beloved plantation worker. The family had lived in a small village on the *motu* of Rimatuu. It was the remnants of their village and the dock used for loading schooners with copra from the coconut grove that I had discovered on that first fateful visit to Tetiaroa during Christmas of 1969.

Tamanu trees have leaves that form a protective canopy against the brilliant tropical sun. Evidently, the trees were planted around 500 years ago by early Tahitians to create shade. They are not native to atolls, suggesting that Tetiaroa had been visited for at least five centuries. Rimatuu is the only one of the thirteen *motus* that had evidence of a recently inhabited village, the one occupied by the Williams/Duran family and their workers. The trees, however, can be found on at least one other *motu*, Onetahi, leading one to think that it too may have had historical significance.

Marlon had learned of Tetiaroa while filming *Mutiny on the Bounty* in 1962. Many of the shots were filmed on the ship which had been built as a replica of the original H.M.S. Bounty. The ship was taken out to the ocean early each morning with a full crew of actors and extras aboard, and maneuvered for a shot with the best background, depending on the scene. This process would take hours and depended on the winds, the sails, the sea, and the weather. Marlon, who liked to sleep late and hated waiting around, refused to board the ship with everyone else so early in the morning. He'd have to be called when the shot was ready to be filmed. Sometimes he couldn't even be found, the naughty boy. So MGM hired Nick Rutgers, who had a speedboat, to ferry Marlon out to the Bounty whenever they were ready to shoot a scene with him in it. Nick, a scion of the Rutgers University family, lived near Papeete and was well tuned in to the "coconut radio" (local gossip). He would find Marlon wherever he had wandered, or was sleeping, and zip him out to the ship.

As they were passing by Tetiaroa on one of those trips, Marlon's jaw dropped as he asked, "What is that?" Nick told him the story of Dr. Williams and Mrs. Duran, and Marlon was intrigued. He asked Nick to take him to the island, and once on shore by zodiac, became instantly enchanted. No one was there, and Marlon thought he had discovered paradise. I can easily relate to that; I had felt the same way on my first visit. Marlon wondered if the atoll was for sale and asked Nick if he could be introduced to Mrs. Duran, who at the time had already moved to Papeete. Alice, Marlon's secretary and confidante, remembers the day that she and Marlon visited Mrs. Duran. "She was old and weak, glad to have visitors, but would not talk about selling the atoll." Marlon became obsessed with buying Tetiaroa and tried his best to charm her, but to no avail. Mrs. Duran died soon after and left the atoll to her daughter. When Marlon found out, he quickly called Mrs. Duran's daughter in Northern California, and turned on the seductive side of his personality once again. He convinced her that he would be a trustworthy and faithful steward of the atoll's legacy, and promised to "preserve the atoll in its natural state as much as is possible," if she would only sell it to him. In the end she did.

I found that there was almost no geographical material available regarding the *motus*, not even a decent map. The atoll had not been surveyed in modern times, and several questions posed themselves immediately. Most important was to find out how much potable water was available. Without water, it would be difficult to do anything at all. We needed to know the sizes of the small *motus* within the lagoon, and how much annual rainfall we could count on. Wind directions and their strengths would be important considerations for construction and the positioning of a possible airstrip. What kind of construction material was available? Could we use local trees as lumber? What was the existing animal life, including rats and mosquitoes, and where were the marshy areas where they could breed? We needed to find the existing archaeological sites, so we could make sure that we did not accidentally disturb them during construction. Seabird colonies and turtle nesting grounds had to be identified and protected. We needed to find a safe and easy access to the atoll during construction, and as soon as possible. It was an enormous project. We could only do so much in the Los Angeles office, and although I had access to the files in Marlon's Los Angeles home, it was clear that I would have to organize a survey trip to the atoll.

That autumn, during the early stages of our research, Marlon happened to be in Los Angeles, and I went to his house on Mulholland Drive frequently. The driveway leading to his and his neighbor, Jack Nicholson's, property was not gated. Marlon's house was a single-story building reminiscent of Japanese architecture. It was surprisingly open, not unlike his house in Tahiti. Friends and associates would enter through the kitchen door unannounced, and just hang around. I never once, in all those years, saw the front door used. Alice was an attractive, elegant, and classy lady. She ran Marlon's L.A. house with the help of Blanche, his long-time, ever-faithful housekeeper. I, too, entered the house through the kitchen. I'd usually find other people there. Among them were his very funny pal Wally Cox, who had his own TV show at the time, or Phil Rhodes, his long-time friend and makeup man, or perhaps Christian Marquand, a debonair old friend from Paris. Reiko Sato, who was a dancer in *Flower Drum Song*, or Jill Banner, a beautiful young actress and protégé of Marlon's, were often there as well. Sometimes Jack Nicholson's girlfriends would just pop in. Over the years, Marlon had many assistants, most of whom were probably also his girlfriends. The one exception was his beloved Alice, who was more like a mother to him and his kids, and who remained at his side until the very end.

Marlon left his home wide open, but he himself stayed hidden away in his bedroom. He almost never left that room. Alice would usher me in and I would find him dressed in a kimono, sitting on his big bed. Sometimes he would stay on that bed the whole time I was there. Other times we would sit opposite each other, me on a small couch, Marlon on an overstuffed chair with a low coffee table between us, examining maps and charts. The room was filled with books, scripts, bongo drums, file cabinets, and even a movie camera aimed straight at the bed. I found that interesting, but never inquired about it. Sliding glass doors opened out to a thick bamboo stand. The room was essentially Marlon's home, office, and refuge all in one. He spent a lot of time on the phone. He knew that he could call almost anyone in the world, anytime, and they would take his call. Sometimes he faked accents and called people he didn't know just to amuse himself. His bedroom was where he seemed to live much of his Los Angeles life; he slept, ate, met people, and did business there. A handwritten sign taped to the bedroom door read: "Do not enter or you will be shot."

Marlon was terrific with accents. He spoke very passable French and some Japanese as well. I recall a day he phoned me at my office and led me to believe that he was Raiko. She told me that she was "secretly in love with me" and that "we had to meet alone." She went on and on, and told me she wanted to perform a certain "oral exercise" on me. I was speechless. "Gotcha," Marlon hollered after awhile. He loved "gotcha" tricks, but I got back at him as often as I could. I remember walking into his bedroom one day and casually saying, "Marlon, there are a bunch of reporters out in the hallway. Do you want me to let them in all at once?"

He came charging out like a bull from his pen, screaming, "I'll kill them!" Gotcha!

It was clear to me, and I was easily able to convince Marlon that I had to go to Tetiaroa and get to know it better. As with any project, I had to investigate each prospective site in detail. He easily understood my point, considering he had admired my research for the Tahiti Safari Club on Moorea. Tetiaroa would be an even bigger challenge, as there were no recent surveys showing the dimensions of the islets or *motus*. The only map Marlon had was from 1907. Furthermore, I knew nothing about its resources, its flora and fauna. Since we had agreed on preserving Tetiaroa's natural beauty, I needed to educate myself in that regard as well. Bottom line: I needed more information. Marlon agreed that I should make the field trip right away. I made up a list of tasks to be accomplished, and he agreed to pay for the trip. I was elated.

Organizing a survey trip to Tetiaroa proved a formidable task. What are atolls anyway? I learned that they are the essence of life on earth, born of fire, sun, and water. They vary in size from 2 to 20 miles across. Tetiaroa is roughly 5 miles wide. The birth of an atoll commences with an eruption from the ocean floor or a sinking of a volcanic island which leaves just enough mass slightly below the surface for the sun to warm the water and organisms like coral to flourish. A high volcanic island may sink under its own weight. The coral, which are microscopic animals, need sunlight to grow, and since they cannot survive in the air, their colonies spread horizontally just below the surface. After thousands of years, and with the action of tides, some coral remains above sea level and dies, leaving its skeletons to form a reef of limestone upon which flotsam and seabirds might land. The washing of waves and storms break the coral down into sand, and as the reef gets larger and wider, part of it becomes a barrier against crashing waves, allowing for a sandy island to be formed. As more and more sand piles on the dead coral base, wind-borne dust and dirt, seabird droppings, and seeds such as coconuts (they can float a thousand miles) all collect atop. With the aid of moisture from occasional mist and rains, vegetation commences. An atoll is born. If, as in the case of Tetiaroa, the barrier reef spreads wide enough, a lagoon is formed inside the protective reef. In fact, Tetiaroa is one of the few atolls in the world where *motus* exist inside a lagoon protected by an encircling barrier reef without any openings or passes through which large fish could enter. Tetiaroa is an entirely enclosed ecological system.

We had to understand as best we could the interdependence of each part of the system: the aquatic life both inside as well as outside of the reef, the living coral itself, and the sea birds that live on the *motus* protected by the reef. Without healthy coral, there would be no reef; no reef, no *motus*; no *motus*, no birds; no seabirds, no tuna fishing for the Tahitians. It was clear, at least to me, that the human needs in Tahiti were directly impacted by the health of Tetiaroa's coral. It was one thing to say "no pollution," but quite another to follow through with it. As soon as anything new invades an ecological system, "pollutants" follow. The more realistic but no less complicated question was which potential pollutants, and how much of them were acceptable before poisons or algae would start killing the coral reef. What about coral "bleaching," which I was starting to hear about? Was it a predator? Was this a natural cycle that comes and goes, or was it a product of industrial waste in the world's oceans that I had learned about from Danielsson? All these questions posed even more questions. I was fascinated, but slightly taken aback by all the knowledge I would need to gain.

Still in Los Angeles, and preparing for the survey trip, we found that each and every task had to be anticipated and thoroughly analyzed in terms of personnel and equipment required. We compiled seemingly endless lists. If certain pieces of equipment were to be lost or broken, what could we use instead? We could not double up on equipment, as this would be too much to carry. Our architectural, engineering, and scientific teams spent hours and hours going over every single detail. We knew that once we were on the atoll, without a radio or any other form of communication, there would be no replacements for missing items. We had long and marvelous "what if..." sessions in the Schindler house garden outside my office. They were a lot of fun, but also critical to our success. How many people do we need to get the research done? How do we get the people and their equipment on the atoll? How long does our investigation take? What if we are there for months at a time? How do we live off the land?

We divided our final lists of equipment and work crews into two separate categories: those available in Tahiti, and those we needed to import from the U.S. I knew we could get a survey crew on Tahiti. I had met a Chinese surveyor named Lee on one of my previous trips. I needed at least one, maybe two laborers to dig wells, cut brush, and act as porters for equipment. Marlon suggested that I take Agnes along. She had been to Tetiaroa with him several times, and she knew the good places for camping. She also knew which *motus* to avoid because of mosquitoes and *nonos*, sand flies. She could identify flora and fauna in both French and Tahitian, plus she would be an all-around happy camper. I estimated that we needed about a week in Tahiti to pre-arrange for transportation, buy food and supplies, as well as cooking and eating utensils, and to gather equipment such as machetes, flashlights, kerosene lamps, flares, soap, picks, and shovels. Once on the atoll, ten days seemed enough time to do all the necessary survey work.

I would take rain and wind gauges, a compass, tents, cameras and film, medical supplies, measuring tapes, sterile bottles for water samples, plastic bags to collect soil samples, and a roll of bright-red plastic sheeting to be used for marking devices. The idea was to place markers on the beach for aerial mapping. I purchased several 1-mile lengths of non-stretch, floatable string in case the surveyors could not measure the lagoon for some reason or other. It took me a week just to locate that string.

I arrived in Papeete in early November, had no trouble getting through customs despite my odd assortment of baggage, and took a cab to Marlon's. He was in England at the time, preparing for the thriller, *The Nightcomers*, and had told me on the phone before he left, "Bernie, I have to go back to work so I can support you and your crazy ideas."

Claude Girard, Marlon's attorney in Tahiti, offered me his superb motorboat, its captain, as well as the captain's mate, Kahuka, a hefty, good-natured Tahitian with powerful shoulders and a dazzling smile. He was from the Tuamotu Islands, where people still had their teeth. Their diet consisted mostly of coconut, taro, fruit, and fish, and had not been contaminated with the likes of Coca-Cola or candy. Kahuka was a terrific fisherman who would supply us with plenty of fresh fish during the trip. Lee, the surveyor I had worked with on Moorea while developing The Tahiti Safari Club with Jack, was available and would bring an assistant. One day, while gathering equipment in Papeete, I asked my friend Zeke at the Bank of Tahiti if he knew a reliable Tahitian I might use as a general helper. "Yes," he replied, "Me. I could use an adventure!" What a perfect idea to bring your personal banker along, and on a project he would later be asked to finance.

Of course Tea just had to come along too, but Zeke and Tea would need a babysitter for their three kids. Michele, the twenty-year-old daughter of Zeke's friend Omer Darr, was taking care of and living on the Fairweather, moored in the Papeete Harbor. Omer, a famous blue water sailing master was out of town at the time. Michele agreed to move to Zeke and Tea's house for the time being and take care of the children. She was quite happy to have a real bathroom for a change. Things were shaping up. Just before departing, I realized that we had no fresh water to take with us. I couldn't believe I was guilty of such a stupid oversight. As it happened, the Fairweather was berthed close by, so I ran over and asked Michele if I could borrow four jerry cans of water, which was about 20 gallons. Michele came to our rescue for the first of many times to come. With the water, we had everyone and everything aboard Claude's boat, including a zodiac with an outboard motor. On a brilliantly sunny morning I shall never forget, off we sailed, bound for Tetiaroa.

Luck was with us. The seas were calm as we approached. My heart was beating with both fear and excitement. I was fearful of the journey across the reef and excited about seeing the atoll again. The mystical appearance of surf and trees in the middle of the ocean cannot be overstated. It is enthralling, at once real and an illusion. It had taken us three hours to get to Tetiaroa. We headed towards the remains of the old copra pier on the reef across from Rimatuu, and anchored 50 yards out. We dropped our inflated zodiac overboard, loaded it up, and got in ourselves. The waves were a foot or two high, and after holding off waiting for a wave to catch us, we rowed like the devil to be carried across the reef. Holding my breath, I thought of what Marlon always said when we went over the Punaruu rapids in Tahiti: "Hang on to your yarmulke, Bernie, here we go!" What a relief it was that we didn't capsize! It took several trips to get all the gear and the crew ashore, but by noon we were done. Claude's boat, which had brought Zeke, Tea, Agnes, two surveyors, Kahuka, and I to the atoll, tooted a salute and was on its way back to Tahiti. It would be ten days before its return. We were on our own.

We had figured that Tetiaroa's lagoon was 4 or 5 miles wide from reef to reef. Standing on the beach, it certainly looked larger. We had made the decision to look for a *motu* wide enough for a small airstrip, at least 600 meters long and in the east-west direction. We needed an "airport," as Marlon and I didn't want to blast a hole in the reef to make a pass large enough for a boat, thereby endangering the ecological balance of the lagoon. While the bay at Rimatuu where we had landed was good for easy off-loading without a pass, we weren't sure if it would make a good permanent port of entry to Tetiaroa, because it was the location of the old village Marlon wanted to preserve. It also didn't seem the right choice for an airstrip. We decided not to camp on the *motu*, as it had a shallow, brackish lake in the middle, and therefore, a lot of mosquitoes.

As far as we could see, the lagoon was only 4 to 8 feet deep. In the clear water between coral heads we spotted all kinds of fish darting about, including small lagoon sharks, which, our Tahitian friends said, would not harm us. While rummaging around the abandoned village, we found an old, beat-up surfboard and an army cot. We managed to attach the cot to the board, creating a double-decker raft that we could tow behind the zodiac with its small 3-horsepower Seagull outboard engine. After loading our supplies on the makeshift raft, we ventured slowly across the shallow lagoon to Motu Onetahi, about 2 miles away. Once safely across, and after unpacking his gear on the beach, Lee yelled, "I forgot my chain!" A chain is what surveyors call a long measuring tape. That tape was necessary to measure the *motus* and the atoll. "Good thing I brought that damn string," I mumbled, clearly concerned, considering this was our very first day.

Once we had set up camp next to the remains of an old copra plantation shed near the beach, we could relax in the soft breeze of the trade winds. Kahuka went fishing, and before we knew it, he came back with a string of fish on his spear. We lit a campfire, opened a bottle of wine, and, forgetting the missing tape for a moment, we toasted our very successful first day on Tetiaroa.

It's hard to describe the sky at night on an unpopulated atoll. Imagine millions of sparks in the ink-black velvet space above. Lying on the beach, one can't help but wonder at the enormity of life and the insignificance of self. I have never experienced such a sense of the universe anywhere else, and I have done more than my share of traveling. As a child traveling to and from France with my mother, I crossed the seas many times, but the steady distracting rumble of the ocean liner's engines, hypnotic as they are, do not allow for contemplation of the universe. On a sailboat, the constant clanging of the rigging and whipping of the sails keep you in this world.

While serving in the Sea Bees in the early 1950s, I lived for three and a half years in French Morocco, and took every opportunity to explore the desert. I experienced the Sahara at night while traveling with Tuareg nomads, but the camels and their mewing were always a presence I could not ignore. Tetiaroa was different. Except for the soothing sound of the gentle lapping of the water, and the slight rustle of the leaves due to ever-blowing trade winds, there was really nothing to remind me of the very real world we live in. It was a deeply emotional experience, and I dreamed that future visitors to Tetiaroa would share this feeling of at-oneness with the universe.

At dawn, I took note of our surroundings. Our camp was located in a small clearing facing the beach, with a view of the lagoon and *motus* a few miles away, and seabirds floating in the sky. The view was toward the east, where the sun rose over the horizon each morning, casting a silver glow on the lagoon. The other three sides of the clearing were composed of dense jungle and coconut trees. In the clearing itself, we found a two-sided structure, perhaps 6 feet square, the roof and walls made of woven coconut leaves. It appeared to have been a kitchen hut, and would serve as the basis for my first architectural lesson on Tetiaroa. Why only two walls? One was toward the dominant breeze, coming from the east. Evidently, that breeze could develop, from time to time, into a strong wind, and a wall was needed for protection. The other wall was on the south, where the cold *maraamu* wind blows hard from the South Pole during certain times of the year. No other walls were needed in a kitchen, only a roof to protect from the rain. So why build what was not absolutely necessary?

We found a second abandoned hut of about 250 square feet. Its structure was composed of coconut posts and rafters from slim local trees. The original raised wood floor above the sand was still intact inside. Thatch made of coconut leaves, *niau*, covered the roof and the 3-foot-high walls. The *niau* was rotting away, but the posts and rafters seemed sturdy enough. Based on the condition of the roof, Kahuka estimated the hut was seven to eight years old. Perhaps a fisherman had rebuilt the roof and lived there for a while. *Niau* roofing, he told us, lasts fewer than ten years. Coconut posts, on the other hand, will last a long time if set on stones or another surface above ground. I was on my way to developing a new and useful Tahitian architectural vocabulary.

Our little clearing, shaded by tall coconut trees and open to breezes and magnificent views, was all I needed to be completely enamored. Terns, black and white, decorated the sky with their quick looping flight, punctuated occasionally by a swift plunge into the lagoon. Coconut trees, with their constantly moving leaves, never let me forget that I was a guest in their world. Their rustling, together with the lapping of the waves on the beach, was a reminder, to me at least, never to interfere with the music of nature. But then, why was I there if not to introduce a discordant note? It was a troubling thought. Was I avaricious, someone who would do anything for a buck? No. Marlon was only paying me the bare minimum, so

The first survey trip arrival: two surveyors, Kahuka, Zeke, Tea, and Agnes.

Next morning: "Oh God, where is the damn surveyor's tape?"

that was not it. Or, was it that, having been given the opportunity to make such natural beauty accessible to others, I would do my utmost not to disturb that completely natural setting? Yes. I wanted the island to be both appreciated and preserved, as did Marlon. A tall order, and worries as to whether I'd be able to actually fulfill that tall order would plague me often. It was not for another two years that I realized with considerable relief that a small plane, flying low, cannot be heard among the natural sounds of the atoll unless you are on the runway itself.

Walking around the island, about a mile in circumference, was very instructive. As I ambled along on that second day, I noticed that each bend had a character of its own. I noted changes in the wind and views, vegetation, the light on the lagoon, and even differences in the sand underfoot. It was coarser on the west and almost rocky on the south, due no doubt to heavy seas and storms accompanying the southern wind, the *maraamu*. On the sunset side, the west, the reef was close and the sound of crashing surf was ever present. It was also several degrees hotter there, as the cooling breezes from the east didn't penetrate the dense foliage in the middle of the *motu*. A vague plan was beginning to form in my mind. It was purely instinctive at first, but this seemed to suit this project better than reason or experience. Anything we'd build here would have to be open to the elements, yet protective, allow for the sensual pleasures of nature, yet remain comfortable for reflection and relaxation. The drama of the sunset would be important. Not only for the colors of the sky and the sea, but also for the light coming through the leaves, changing them from green to yellow and even gold as the sun settled over the horizon. I was happy knowing that eventually others would be able to share the delights of wandering and wondering on Tetiaroa.

Our primary task in those first few days was to measure the width of the *motu* from east to west, and note the direction of the dominant trade winds. In hacking through the jungle, the surveyors had to start a small fire in order to smoke out some bees from a thick bush in their path. Before they knew it, the fire had spread out of control, and they yelled for help. As I ran up, I thought, "This is just great! First week on the island and we burn it down!" Agnes quickly arrived with a bottle of Evian and sprinkled its contents on the flaming bush. I wondered what she was doing. Did she honestly think that would help put out the fire? But at that very moment, the skies opened up and a tremendous rain shower came down on us and extinguished the flames. Agnes stood there laughing. She had seen the rain cloud and knew how fast it would burst. It was a Tahitian version of "gotcha!"

After a lot of traveling back and forth across the lagoon to the other *motus*, I determined that because of its size and orientation toward the dominant wind, Onetahi was the best location for an airstrip. Our next challenge was to find out how much fresh water was available on Onetahi. The paramount factor controlling population density on atolls is the amount and

Tea organizing camp.

Photo by MR

Top
Our first breakfast.

Bottom
Zeke and I are happy campers.

Me at my improvised drafting board.

quality of fresh water, which can come from two sources: rainwater catchments and ground water. If ground water can be considered a storage reservoir, the necessity and expense of catching and storing large amounts of water above ground is reduced. It was time to put theory into practice.

I had done my homework on the Ghyben-Herzberg principle Roby had mentioned. The hydrology of atolls is based on the fact that the permeability of the dead coral substrata absorbs large amounts of water. This water, both salt and fresh, makes up a substantial percentage of the ground volume of the atoll. The principle states that the ratio of the depth of fresh water below sea level to the height of the fresh water above sea level is also the ratio of specific gravities of one to the other. Since that ratio is 40:1, the depth of sea water below sea level could be calculated by a careful measurement of fresh water above sea level. Fortunately, the level of the lagoon on each side of our *motu* did not fluctuate very much, as there are practically no tides in this part of the world. I therefore knew it would be possible to make the calculations.

Two other factors come into play. Gravity tends to cause lateral flow away from the center of the island. Since more salt water is displaced in the middle than at the edges, a water table is formed, shaped like a lens. Also, rainfall fluctuations affect the fresh water lens. Given the rainfall and the level of the fresh water above sea level, one can closely approximate the amount of fresh water in the lens. The idea was for us to dig twenty holes to the depth of the water table in a grid throughout the island. Then we would measure the height of the water table compared to the lagoon water level. Using the 40:1 ratio, we could chart the depth of the fresh water lens in plan as well as in section. For every centimeter of fresh water above the lagoon level there would be 40 centimeters of fresh water floating on seawater below. We would take samples of the water we found, as well as samples of ground material and sand from the holes that we dug. Both the water and ground samples were to be taken to a laboratory in Papeete for testing. Zeke was in charge of the digging — good exercise for a banker — and I did the plotting and measuring. We found that after a day of settling its solids, the fresh water was drinkable. No one who tried it got sick. There's nothing like being one's own guinea pig. We also drank from a 50-gallon drum we had found had filled with rainwater. The insides of the drum were coated with moss and furry green algae, but if one was careful not to disturb the water while dipping it out with a cup made out of half a coconut, it tasted flat but quite good.

We set up rain gauges. These would, of course, be long-term measurements over a period of years. Rain on an atoll is somewhat unusual. Atolls are flat and have no mountains to attract clouds. The oceanic trade winds carry moisture that has evaporated from the sea, but clouds go floating right by atolls looking for mountain peaks. Once clouds congregate around mountains, they produce rain that encourages the growth of vegetation, which then turns evaporation into more clouds. The cycle can be considered in reverse. Clouds drift over atolls. Fewer clouds cause less rain, resulting in less vegetation, which, in turn, limits evaporation and less rain. It's a bleak situation for vegetation. Only the heartiest plants can exist on an atoll. Rainwater is limited to the occasional squall. But a surprising number of plants do exist, and even thrive.

This was my second time on Tetiaroa. I often thought of Marlon's initial words: "The island is beautiful beyond my capacity to describe, or cinematography to capture. Its spirit can only be experienced by being there." I couldn't agree more. There is nothing in the world like being on a long, isolated beach in the sun. It makes you want to take off your clothes and run in the sand, your toes dug into its soft texture, or your feet bouncing on the wet, compact sand at the water's edge. And that is exactly what we did whenever we had a chance. At least Tea, Zeke, and I did. The rest of the crew, being Tahitian, was used to being half naked. They just liked being in the peace and quiet of the island, away from the relative hustle-bustle of Papeete, and marveling at us *popaas* going wild on the beach. I can still see Tea in my mind's eye, her naked skin bronzed, disheveled brown hair blowing in the breeze, elegantly loping along, happy and free. We all were part of and in tune with the forces around us, the soft winds rustling leaves in the trees, the music of the waves in the sea. I would not exchange this experience for anything in the world.

The surveyors, when not setting fires, were still trying to map the lagoon, but with little success. Our floating string would not stay in a straight line for a mile in length. The lagoon actually has a slight current. The windward side empties into the leeward side and the current intensifies between *motus*, making our string idea ultimately useless. We had to find another way to measure the lagoon.

Tea hunted for obvious archeological sites on all the *motus*. She found two on Onetahi. One site, composed of several coral slabs standing upright in the middle of the jungle, she recognized as backrests, an indication of a *marae*, an ancient place of worship. Agnes jotted down the names of plants and animals that she came across on the island. We were looking for trees that could be used as lumber and she identified the hardwood *tamanu*, ironwood (*aito*), breadfruit (*uru*), and, of course, the coconut tree (*haari*). Its wood is good for making posts and planks, and its leaves for thatch (*niau*). She also found pandanas plants (*fara*), which, she knew, had leaves good for roof thatch, floor mats, or wall coverings. Hibiscus, gardenia, frangipani, and papaya were known by her to be imported plants, perhaps from Tahiti.

By the ninth and final afternoon, we had pretty much positioned the best location for an airstrip. After checking its length, orienting it in line with the dominant wind and staking it out, we called it a day, our final one of the survey. At dinner that night, Tea remembered a cluster of large *tamanu* trees that she knew were usually associated with human activity. There was such a cluster very close to the end of where we had determined the airstrip should be. To be certain, the whole crew set out with flashlights to see if there might be an archaeological site near the trees. Cutting through the brush in darkness, we found, to our dismay, that Tea had been absolutely right. The trees were at the end of the runway. We could not make the strip shorter; there was not an inch to spare across the length of the island. So I moved the orientation of the airstrip 5 degrees off course, aiming the runway a bit cross wind in order to avoid the trees which were growing in a possible archaeological site. To this day, due to Tea's find, airplanes approach at an angle to the airstrip, and at the very last moment, have to line up the plane and land. Pilots still curse me!

We had had the opportunity, thanks to our Tuamotu fisherman, to catalogue aquatic life in the lagoon, as well as to spot five different seabird colonies and two nesting grounds for turtles. In addition to lagoon sharks, manta rays, parrotfish, red snapper, mullet, sand dabs, surgeonfish, clown and damselfish, spiny lobsters, and an assortment of clams, he identified a large mantis shrimp with a transparent carapace, or shell, that the Tahitians call *varo*. These shrimp are practically extinct on other islands, as they are caught for their delicate, sweet flavor. We were excited to have found them on Tetiaroa. We collected hermit crabs, sand crabs, and coconut crabs, which are huge, bright-blue crustaceans that feed on coconuts. We ate a lot of these, and I couldn't believe how delicious they were. Sideways-walking land crabs that are called *tupas* were plentiful but inedible. We didn't eat any rats, lizards, or geckos, although there were lots of them too.

Tetiaroa is renowned for its seabird colonies. They are an important resource for the fishing industry, as they identify the location of tuna and other large ocean fish for fishermen. The birds circle in swarms looking for schools of small fish, which swim close to the surface, trying to escape the mouths of the larger fish below. When a fisherman sees the diving birds, he knows that tuna can be found below. On a couple of *motus,* we found colonies of frigates and terns, and brown and red-footed boobies by the thousands. And we spotted one heron during our stay. We quickly realized that the bird colonies and nesting grounds, as well as those of the sea turtles, would have to be preserved.

Due to the fact that we could not map the atoll accurately without a surveyor's tape, and only poorly with our inadequate string method, we positioned 1-meter-square red plastic markers exactly 1 mile apart on several beaches to be used in aerial surveys. Before leaving the atoll, we set rain and wind gauges for future reference. All in all, we had a successful trip. We had not only survived — we had eaten gloriously well, made fascinating archaeological discoveries, done some solid initial work, laughed a good deal, swum in our lagoon, and also gotten to know each other under sometimes trying circumstances. Work had been difficult at times, cutting through thick brush or digging holes in the heat. Measuring the lagoon had proven hopeless, and there were language and cultural barriers to be overcome. We were a disparate group: a young American banker and his beautiful Tahitian wife out for an adventure; a Chinese surveyor and his Tahitian assistant; a fisherman from the Tuamotu Archipelago; a Tahitian woman who had recently lost her Chilean lover, probably there to report back to Marlon; and last but not least, a young (well, maybe not so young) American architect who was learning as he went along, and loving every minute of it. One must not forget that none of the members of this team, except for the two surveyors and me, were being paid! It was with great regret that, when the boat appeared on the horizon to take us back to Tahiti, we folded camp and set out back across the lagoon.

When I returned to Papeete, my last important task was to make an aerial photographic survey of Tetiaroa, using the red markers we'd left on the beach to provide us with a scale to work from. I found a plane with a removable piece of metal on its floor. It could be unscrewed, leaving an open space at its bottom for a camera. I hitched my 35mm camera over the open space, and, seated and straddling the opening with one foot on either side, I shot hundreds of pictures as we flew back and forth across the atoll in a prescribed pattern and at a level of exactly 2,000 feet. The pictures would provide us with an absolutely true picture of what the atoll looked like from the air: its size, shape, plant life, and even lagoon depth, which could be calculated according to color. When I returned to Los Angeles, developed the pictures, and projected the slides, I was able to trace the first fairly accurate map of the Tetiaroa atoll. The feeling of accomplishment was remarkable.

Top
A young booby living on one of the motus.

Bottom
Dr. William's wife's grave on Motu Rimatuu.

We found upright coral slabs in the middle of the island.

Top
We found all sorts of fish in the lagoon.

Bottom
I had never seen a coconut crab before.

Top
Terns live on certain motus.

Bottom
The booby chick was not afraid of us.

Top
We saw thousands of boobies.

Bottom
Birds laid their eggs right on the sand.

Top
We found turtles in the lagoon.

Bottom
The reef was full of colorful clams (paua).

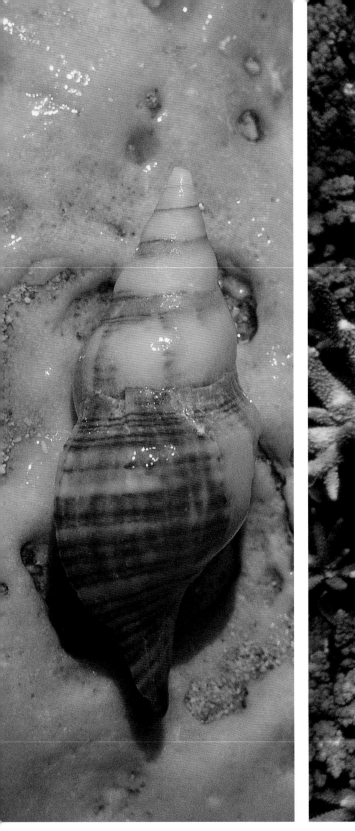

Left
Beautiful shell.

Right
Colorful reef life.

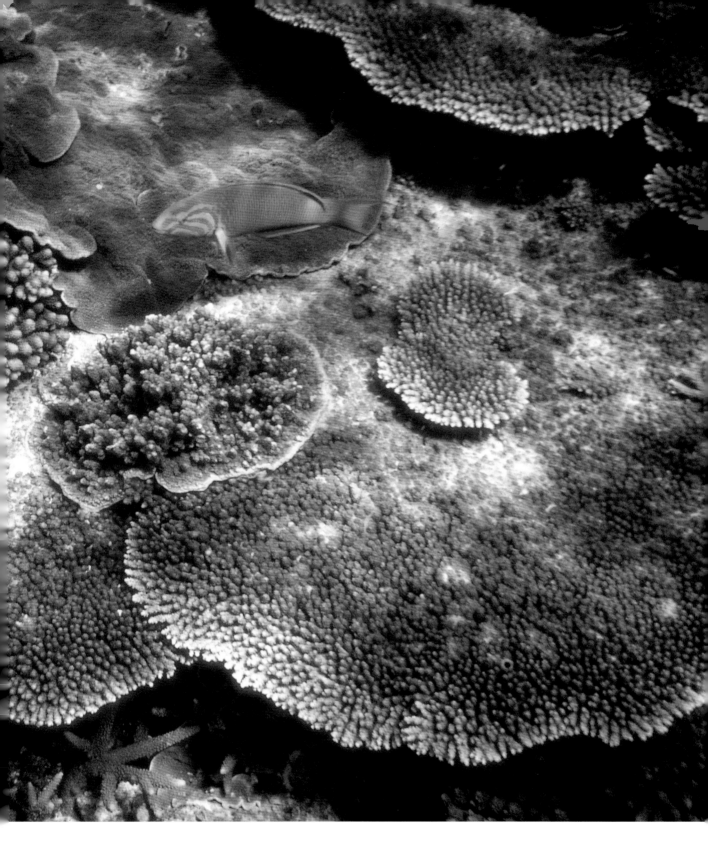

Last dawn from our campsite.

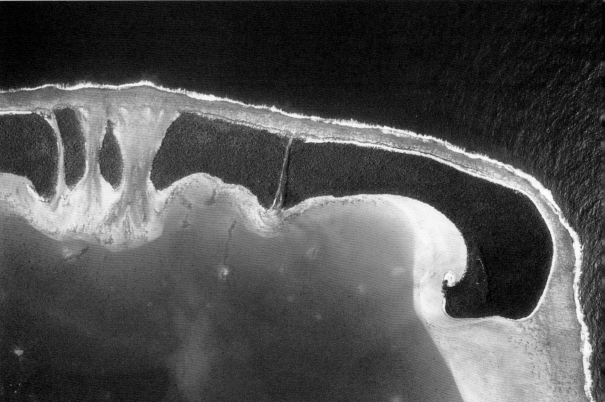

Top
Setting out to leave paradise.

Bottom
Aerial mapping, one of 200 photos.

Views from our first aerial survey.

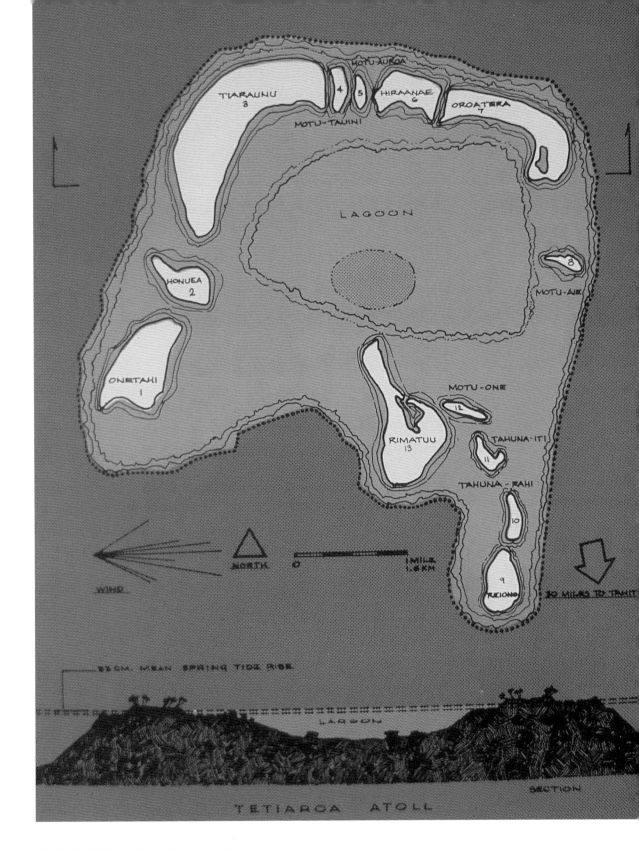

TIARAUNU
3

MOTU-AUROA

4 5 HIRAANAE
6

OROATERA
7

MOTU-TAVINI

LAGOON

HONUEA
2

8

MOTU-AIE

ONETAHI
1

MOTU-ONE

12

TAHUNA-ITI

RIMATUU
13

11

TAHUNA - RAHI

NORTH   0   1 MILE
                     1.6 KM

10

WIND

9
TAEIONO

30 MILES TO TAHITI

23 CM. MEAN SPRING TIDE RISE

LAGOON

SECTION

TETIAROA ATOLL

My first plan of Tetiaroa drawn after the survey trip.

A MASTER PLAN

How to Do It If You've Never Done It Before

After coming back from the survey trip and taking into consideration all I had learned, I began to question Marlon's early concept of building a first-class hotel. Somehow, "first-class" seemed to go against the realities of the site. Marlon's first impulse had been to do something grand. At the same time, he wanted the atoll free of pollution. I wondered how we would control the impact of such a large project and its necessary infrastructure on the idyllic, untouched paradise that Tetiaroa was. Keeping the environment free of negative impacts would require a small fortune, and that fortune would have to be repaid by a large and wealthy clientele. The atoll would ultimately be for the rich and famous. Is that what Marlon really wanted? Or was Hawaii, with its grand hotels, the model we should follow? They attracted mass tourism, and had positive effects on the economy, and as far as I knew at that time, had little negative effect on the environment. My personal favorite was the Mauna Kea on the Big Island of Hawaii. It was glorious and located on a beautiful site; I would have died to design something on such a grand scale. But in my heart, I knew that a grand hotel was not right for Tetiaroa.

I voiced my concerns to Marlon, and we talked about alternatives. I brought up Tree Tops in Kenya, a rough-hewn hotel set in the trees above a watering hole. It had been built for Queen Elizabeth's visit to the Kenyan game reserves in the 1950s. I also mentioned the Club Med Moorea — a couple of central structures surrounded by small thatch huts set in flowering gardens. Since we had been discussing housing the hotel employees as well, a village atmosphere of thatch bungalows seemed to be closer to the mark than a large hotel complex.

I suggested we visit the Club Med. Marlon had never been there. We flew to Moorea, and to my pleasant surprise, his prominence did not cause a stir. We strolled about the gardens amid the A-frame huts. They were so close together that privacy was not always guaranteed. Walking between them, Marlon commented, "Hear that, Bernie, they're fucking in that one. Jeez, she's having a good one." He crept close, holding a make-believe microphone. "OK, roll tape." I was holding my belly laughing, hoping that no one could hear him, while making a mental note about the space required for privacy between bungalows. We had lunch at a long communal table in the dining hall. We stood in line with the other guests at a sumptuous buffet and sat on benches at the next free table, as directed by a *pareo*-draped hostess. There were twelve of us at the table. Of course, Marlon wanted to learn as much as possible and asked a barrage of questions. He kept it up, non-stop, all through lunch, so much so that no one was able to ask him anything about Hollywood or movies. Asking questions incessantly was usually Marlon's way of keeping people at a distance.

Our visit had been a great success in spite of his one comment upon leaving: "You made your point, Bernie. The village concept will work on Tetiaroa, and a buffet with food from our own gardens and lagoon is just great, but a hostess telling us where to sit — that sucks!"

Marlon and I had very few disagreements during our discussions about the Master Plan. We were in sync, perhaps because I insisted that the ideas as they presented themselves had to be based in reality, both his and mine, rather than on fantasy, his or mine.

The further I got, the more I realized that designing a community from scratch on a deserted island is a daunting challenge. I had to make it right from a physical, social, and financial perspective, and frankly, I felt a little scared. I had started by identifying Marlon's main goals, which were to create a self-sustaining community, including housing for Marlon, his family, and friends; a visitation program for the public; and a marine research and training center. All this had to be accomplished within sound ecological constraints. Initially, we had very little money to work with, and Marlon did not want to have financial partners or incur large debts. We had to start small. The estimated budget for the airstrip, for example, was $30,000. In fact, it ended up costing $100,000.

Using the data I had collected on the survey trip, we settled on Motu Onetahi as the best location for the airstrip and therefore for the hotel/village. We also decided on two of the larger *motus* as possible locations for nutriculture and aquaculture projects, and on certain smaller *motus* as natural refuges for the seabirds that inhabit Tetiaroa. Finally, we selected Rimatuu, the site of Dr. William's former home, as the best place for a marine research station. The existing lake and the proximity to the ocean was perfect for marine research, and we felt that the nearby skeleton of an old wharf could be rebuilt. Therefore, Rimatuu was chosen as the proper point for access from the sea.

The First Phase

We developed a two-phase program for the implementation of Marlon's plans. Phase one would include providing access to the atoll, building a village (including a small hotel), starting food production (fish farming and growing vegetables), and setting up day tours for visitors. The latter was a necessity, because the small amount of tourism (we called it "visitation") would provide some much-needed income.

It was clear that the barrier reef would have to remain untouched. Primary access to Tetiaroa had to be by air, and therefore our first task was to build the airstrip. As Onetahi was farthest from seabird nesting grounds, we had one more good reason to build both the airstrip and the village there. Two key elements of the first phase were satisfied. The lagoon would not be compromised, and access to the atoll would be controlled.

Marlon and I had agreed that a working village, open for visitation, rather than a high-priced traditional hotel, would be more in tune with the natural life on Tetiaroa. Due to the overall fragility of the atoll's ecosystems, we decided not to allow any permanent structures on *motus* other than Onetahi. Each building in a traditional Polynesian village has a distinct function. Ours would be comprised of a community of buildings, including sleeping huts, a central dining room, a kitchen, a sanitary building, a beach bar, and small ancillary structures. A reception building with an office and a radio-telephone would be right at the airstrip. Sleeping huts with baths were to be situated in small clearings near the lagoon, spaced far enough apart for privacy, yet in close proximity to the village center. Facilities for day tour groups would include toilets and showers, boats for touring the lagoon and outlying *motus*, and picnic grounds on a secluded beach.

Collecting scientific data was an integral part of the planning process. We wanted to have a record of the ecological conditions before, as well as after, development began, in order

Marlon living his dream.

Top
Marlon cruises the atoll's lagoon.

Bottom
Marlon and me.

Marlon opening up a coconut (the wrong way) with Rosette Valente and friend.

Top
Marlon makes a hat for Rosette.

Bottom
Alice sunning herself.

to understand our long-term impact. Marlon was willing to pay for the initial studies, but we agreed that, given the opportunity, the scientific community would probably be more than happy to have a laboratory on Tetiaroa, and Marlon would simply pay to get them there. In the future, professors and students doing fieldwork would help keep the hotel occupied at modest room rates; I was able to arrange for several scientific and archaeological studies to be conducted, even during the construction years of 1972 and '73.

Our food production plan was theoretical. Marlon had already attracted experienced nutriculture and aquaculture consultants to Tetiaroa, but after careful consideration, we learned that the energy required for infrastructure — pumps, for example — would be too expensive at the very outset of the project. Though the lagoon had a plentiful supply of fish, it could not sustain the impact of fishing to feed a village of what we estimated to be about 100 people every day. Therefore, food for Marlon, his guests, visitors, and employees would have to be imported from Papeete, at least during the first phase, until we'd have the healthy income needed to generate an energy source for our own food production.

We looked into both wind generators and photovoltaic (PV) panels. The latter absorb the sun's energy and transform it into electricity. Neither was economical back then. Our inability to make use of natural sources of energy was a big disappointment for Marlon and me. It was our first major setback during the planning process. We were stuck with the only energy source available at the time, diesel generators. We would have to import diesel fuel, which was both expensive and difficult to bring to the atoll. You can't fly it in. Fifty-gallon drums of diesel had to be brought in by boat. As it turned out, the only way to get them on the atoll was rather labor-intensive. The drums had to be dropped overboard from fishing boats. They would float until swimmers would push them into the surf and onto the reef, and then across the lagoon. Not a very elegant solution! Every once in a while a drum would get away. There are probably fuel drums with "BRANDO" painted on them floating somewhere in the Pacific today, ready to explode.

The size of the village was to be controlled by the quantity and quality of the fresh water available. The water in the lens turned out to be not only safe to drink, but also plentiful enough that, at 250 gallons per person per day, it could support about 100 permanent residents on the *motu*. I based these numbers on the water allowance per guest per day used by the Club Med Moorea, even though statistics at the time claimed Americans were using an average of only 200 gallons per person per day. I thought it prudent to build in a safety net, particularly since the conditions on Tetiaroa were similar to those on Moorea.

Turning seawater into drinking water was theoretically possible. The reverse osmosis technology was being used elsewhere in the world. But forcing seawater through a series of filters requires high pressure, which requires a lot of energy. Due to our limited energy resources, we could not afford this, at least not for the time being.

Marlon's house was to be a hut just like the others, though slightly removed from the village. As much as possible, the huts were to be made of local materials. We'd have huts with thatched-roofs supported by coconut posts, and walls made of woven coconut leaves. Initially, I wanted the floors to be sand, but Marlon convinced me that concrete would be easier to keep clean. And, by the way, he said, visitors might not think to wipe the sand off their feet and would end up with a veritable beach in their beds. Imagine what would happen while making love. Apparently, he was speaking from experience. I was not.

The village would have to have a permanent staff. They would be housed in the same type of facility as the guests. It would be up to the staff person whether they'd be mingled with or apart from the village. Construction materials used in Tahiti still come from overseas, mostly from the U.S., and are therefore very expensive. It made no sense for us to import wood from California when we had our own forest. Instead, we imported a sawmill. Since we knew that our local construction materials, particularly thatch, would not last long, we planned to have a small construction crew on hand for maintenance and refurbishment.

A maintenance building would house utilities systems such as water pumps, electric generators, construction and maintenance equipment, spare parts, and a mulching machine for composting.

Pest control was going to be one of our biggest problems. Marlon had had studies done by experts in the field, and their expensive advice can be summed up in four words: **keep the site clean**. There were three pests on Onetahi that needed to be controlled: rats, flies, and mosquitoes. Fortunately, Motu Onetahi had been a well-managed coconut grove. The trees had been banded, so rats were unable to climb the trunks in order to eat the nuts. The few remaining rats would be dealt with by keeping garbage sealed in containers, and by making sure that food was not left out in the open. Rats and mosquitoes have a symbiotic relationship. Rats gnaw holes into coconuts, where water collects, which provides a ready breeding place for mosquito larvae. The rats themselves provide warm-blooded hosts for the grown mosquitos. We would have to get rid of open coconuts, and the coconuts in the grove had to be collected, and not left to rot or to be eaten by rats. We also would have to be careful not to inadvertently import rats from Motu Rimatuu, next to the old copra-loading pier, which we used for unloading supplies. It had a large population of healthy rats, as well as mosquitoes, which happily bred at the large, brackish pond. Fortunately, Onetahi had no pond, but prevailing winds instead. I had sent samples of our mosquitoes to two mosquito experts at the University of California at Berkeley. They found that the species on Tetiaroa do not fly well in the wind, and do not live more than four or five days. We hoped they would not be able to migrate from Rimatuu. As long as standing water was not available in fallen and cracked coconuts, or plant axels that collect water, mosquitoes would not breed.

We surmised that mosquitoes would not be a serious problem, because the village would be facing the wind, and we'd keep it clear of standing water. History, however, would prove us wrong. Years later, many ornamental flowering plants were imported, providing ready breeding grounds in their leaf axels. You should, but you cannot think of everything.

Flies breed in garbage. They are also attracted to fish odors. Cleanliness was the only answer yet again, as pesticides were verboten. Pesticides were bound to seep into the ground water with the advent of rain, and eventually they'd affect the lagoon and the coral reef beyond. In line with the most important tenet of the plan, pesticides were out.

The financial feasibility of the project was built around day tours and the small hotel operation consisting of twelve bungalows. The construction of the airstrip and initial village was to be financed through a modest bank loan. As we had to delay raising vegetables and farming fish to sell in Papeete to the second phase, initially we had to count solely on paying visitors to finance the project.

The Second Phase

Phase two of the Master Plan would include the building of a school for the employees' children. The school building would also serve as a rental facility for scientists and their fieldwork classes. Aquaculture, fish farming for mullet and shrimp, was to begin on Rimatuu, where the existing lake could be utilized. The culturing of pearls and the farming of turtles were to be considered. Nutriculture, vegetable gardening without good soil and plentiful fresh water, had also been postponed to the second phase. As it turned out, except for the building of the schoolhouse, aquaculture and nutriculture had to be ultimately discarded due to the high costs of electricity required.

Including the preliminary research, I had spent almost two years in discussions with Marlon. I spent an additional three months working practically day and night writing and drawing, assembling, and analyzing data. Once I'd gathered all photos, maps, scientific data, plans, and renderings of what we wanted to build, including a rough cost estimate, we bound it all together. I ended up with one final document, and proudly called it the Master Plan.

Late one night, I arrived at Marlon's house on Mulholland Drive, excited to show it to him. I found him in the bedroom as usual. "Marlon," I said, "here it is. This is what I think we can do on Tetiaroa." He answered, "Looks long. Why don't you read it to me." Marlon was dyslexic and read with difficulty. So we went into the dining room, sat down at the table, and I began to read:

"The Atoll of Tetiaroa, uninhabited and privately owned by Marlon Brando, presents a unique opportunity for enlightened and orderly development. Its climate, geographic location, proximity to Tahiti, its amenities and human resources in the Polynesian people, all constitute a natural living laboratory for insight into the interdependent relationship between the animal world (of which man is a part), the ocean, and a coral atoll. Furthermore, Tetiaroa, if properly developed, will provide the rapidly urbanizing world with the rare experience of living life in a flowering tropical garden, surrounded by clear lagoons, sharing the delights of nature with a stimulating population of working residents. It will stand as an example of an original and creative venture, a haven for artists, scientists, and intellectuals. For it is the objective of this Master Plan to establish on Tetiaroa a self-supporting community, a blending of research and training, nutriculture, aquaculture, and tourism within sound ecological constraints for the particular benefit of the French Polynesian people and the general benefit of all."

I read him the entire Master Plan from start to finish. It took several hours, and he listened intently. Prior to that night, Marlon had often become so engrossed in details that he would miss the larger picture. This was the first time he was able to fully grasp how the atoll should be developed. He smacked me on the back and said, "Okay, great, Bernie, take it down to the governor." Although I knew full well that it all could fall apart if Governor Angelli, who represented the French government, would not approve, I couldn't wait to go. I was immensely proud of my presentation as Marlon, grinning, shook my hand. "Bernie, we're a go!"

I was determined to make it all happen. I flew back to Papeete and gave a leather-bound copy of the Master Plan to Governor Angelli, who looked at me with amusement, and said: "Marlon Brando is a dreamer, but you have my blessing." I showed it to the head of Civil Aviation, who had to approve the proposed airstrip. He said, "Marlon is a dreamer, but I wish you good luck." When I showed it to Alec Ata at the Tourist Development Board, he said, "Looks good, but what are you going to do about water?" Feeling myself to be an expert on these matters, I told him about dogs lapping up fresh water right on the beach. Alec responded, "You may have the first drink, my dear." Then he added, laughingly, "Brando is a dreamer, but go ahead, I support you."

Much later I found out that when a Frenchman calls a person a "dreamer," he doesn't mean a person who dreams. He means a person who is out of his mind!

Top and top right
Sketches of possible types of construction.

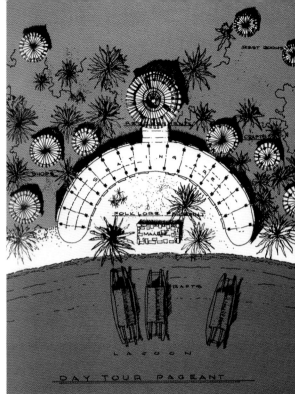

DAY TOUR PAGEANT

Bottom right
Agnes, who escorted me to the governor's office.

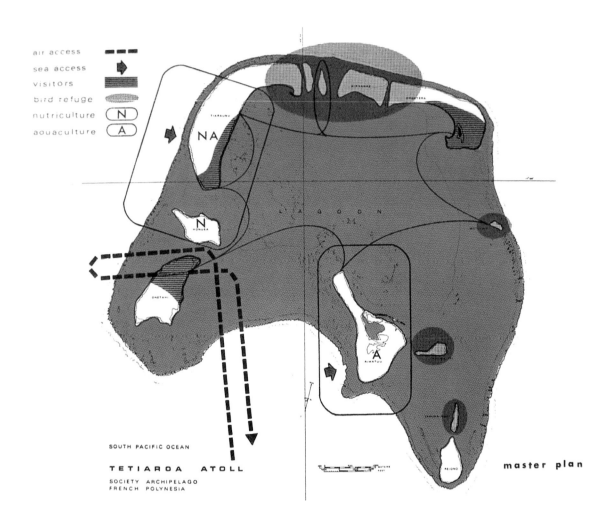

air access
sea access
visitors
bird refuge
nutriculture   N
aquaculture   A

NA

N

A

L A G O O N

SOUTH PACIFIC OCEAN

TETIAROA ATOLL
SOCIETY ARCHIPELAGO
FRENCH POLYNESIA

master plan

The Master Plan.

Sketches of possible buildings.

MAC JOHNSON

January 1972

FINDING A CONTRACTOR

Pot Brownies and Slurping Urchins
The Last Tango

The plans for the Tetiaroa airstrip were finished and we had acquired the permits to build it. We now had to find a local contractor to do the job. There weren't many to choose from. Most of them were either small independent companies doing mostly residential work, or very large French firms experienced with commercial or government projects, many at the atomic testing site near the Moruroa Atoll nearly 800 miles away. The French had been conducting nuclear tests there since 1966. Although the testing was done under water, not in the air, and therefore less likely to produce radiation dangers to populated areas, there was considerable worry that migrating fish might carry radiation across the globe. A world movement opposing testing in the Pacific developed, and finally was able to force France to halt its operations in 1996. Construction at the nuclear test sites had mostly been completed by the time I was looking for contractors, and I hoped to be able to choose among the many contractors that had succumbed to its lure and stayed in Tahiti.

It would take several months to find a contractor for the airstrip and the village. I interviewed several large French contractors in order to find out how they would approach the two projects. However, all French companies proved too costly. In addition, they were used to working with large equipment that would be difficult to bring to the island without harming portions of the reef, or worse, blasting a hole through the reef. And many of the contractors I interviewed were not used to using materials found on the atoll. Locally produced materials from Tahiti, except for the *pandanus* and *niau* used for roofing, had recently been abandoned for newer, imported materials. The irony was that the lumber being imported to Papeete for construction purposes came from the United States. It made me laugh; here I was in the South Pacific, and wood was being imported from California!

Prior to my arrival, the Tahitian government had begun several reforestation programs on the islands, but the wood was not yet mature enough to be used. We learned that some trees they planted were simply the wrong species for construction. The Tahitian reforestation programs were well intended, but the people involved didn't have the experience to establish a proper lumber industry. I found it odd that the French could easily detonate atomic bombs in French Polynesia, but didn't have the foresight to start a lumber industry. A lumber industry would have saved them a lot of money on imports at the very least. Hardwoods such as mahogany, teak, rosewood, and ironwood grow in Polynesia. Likewise, soft woods like cedar that grow relatively fast and straight can be grown in the tropics. Bamboo grows naturally in Tahiti's valleys. It seemed to me that this would make for a strong and healthy industry. Bamboo grows very quickly; it is strong and very beautiful. Bamboo is used as a main construction material throughout Asia. But in Tahiti, I couldn't find anyone who was growing bamboo commercially. A person would have to locate a stand of bamboo on private property, and get the owner's approval to cut and use it. In retrospect, perhaps the French had foresight after all. A lumber industry without proper management and environmental safeguards might denude land, cause erosion, silt lagoons, and harm coral reefs. I wonder if that's why there wasn't one in Tahiti.

Because they had to generate electricity on Moruroa, the French had become expert in photovoltaic (PV) research. After atomic testing had been cut way back, France decided to share with the Tahitians some of the technology they had developed. In the mid-1970s, a center for PV instruction was set up and opened to the public. People on the outer islands were able to get free PV panels for their houses, providing them with inexpensive electricity. This was the first time that I know of that any government actually gave away PV systems. The panels produced very low voltage, and so the government had to support and subsidize the development of special low-voltage washing machines, refrigerators, lighting, and even TVs. When these appliances became available at a reasonable cost, things changed in a big way. Tahitians suddenly had rapid access to the outside world and its technology.

The idea behind making electricity available had been to offer a more comfortable lifestyle to people on the outer islands. But it actually had the opposite effect. As the younger generation became more and more familiar with other ways of life via radio and TV, they discarded the simple, self-sufficient lifestyle. During the early 1980s, many young people left the outer islands and moved to Papeete, where they found themselves untrained and unemployed. There was nothing for them to do. Unemployment rates were unusually high. The unemployed youngsters found themselves cut off from the traditional family support system. The outer islands were simply too far away to stay connected. Theft escalated. The age of Tahitian innocence had ended. Before the 1970s, there had been little or no theft in Tahiti because people were so family-oriented and self-sustaining. People trusted each other, and there was no need to lock up one's belongings. A major social shift was taking place. People began building houses with doors and windows, and they locked them. The government program, intended to improve Tahitian lifestyle, had in fact aided in its demise.

During our search for a contractor, Marlon remembered that when *Mutiny on the Bounty* was being filmed, he'd met a building contractor named Jimmy Nordoff, the son of Charles Nordoff who, together with James Norman Hall, wrote *Mutiny on the Bounty*, the book upon which the film was based. Nordoff and Hall, like many American artists and writers, were drawn to the South Pacific after World War I. They had flown together in the Lafayette Escadrille, a French Air Service made up of American pilots who volunteered to fight the Germans even before the U.S. entered the war in 1917. After the war, both men ended up in Tahiti, where they each married a local girl, had families, and began a collaboration that would last a lifetime. Their South Pacific trilogy — *Mutiny on the Bounty, Men Against the Sea,* and *Pitcairn's Island* — became bestsellers. James Norman Hall remained in Tahiti for the rest of his life.

Conrad Hall, James' son, became a world-renowned cinematographer. "Connie" was raised in Tahiti, and as a young man was sent to America, where he studied film at USC. He ended up earning ten Oscar nominations, winning them for *Butch Cassidy and the Sundance Kid, American Beauty,* and *Road to Perdition*. Marlon met Conrad while shooting *Mutiny on the Bounty*. They became fast friends, and in 1964, Marlon arranged for Connie to shoot his first feature, *Morituri,* in which Marlon and Yul Brynner starred. Marlon introduced me to Connie in the early 1970s and we became life-long pals. I will always remember with great fondness the three of us sharing hilarious semi-truthful stories, told in a mixture of Tahitian, French, and English, while sipping rum punches on the beach.

I got in touch with Jimmy Nordoff, and he, Marlon, and I had lunch together. Jimmy and his crew had gone to great lengths to make sure that we had a special and truly traditional meal. They had gone out early in the morning to collect sea urchins (*vana*) by the dozens; then they scraped out the innards and threw them in a huge bowl. They also marinated fresh tuna in seawater, and let it rot in the sun. A sauce of fermented coconut milk and dead fish (*mitehue*) was whipped together and the meal was complete. We ate it all, dipping our fingers into the bowl and scooping out the slimy urchin, which slipped through our fingers as we slurped it up. We ate the rotten fish holding our noses. It was all we could do to get it down our throats; it smelled like a latrine. We dipped pieces of taro root into the *mitehue* and washed it all down with rum and lime juice. Marlon was sick for three days afterward. Needless to say, Jimmy didn't get the job.

Marlon and I took several prospective contractors to Tetiaroa. I clearly remember one trip with a particular Tahitian contractor. The Zodiac's outboard motor had quit in the middle of the lagoon. We all looked at each other, scratching our heads, wondering what to do next. We either had to swim ashore or push the boat, or both. The contractor lifted the cowling off the motor and looked inside. He smiled up at everyone, took off his belt, and replaced the cotter pin with his belt buckle. The engine started up, and we were off again with the belt trailing behind us like a sea snake. On the way home that night, Marlon said to me, "We're not going to use that guy. He's either too clever or that belt thing was a set-up. Either way, he'd probably try to screw me."

We finally found the contractor who would build our airstrip, Teari Taputuarai. I was happy to have found a local contractor rather than a Frenchman, and Teari was extremely well qualified. His crew was from the outer islands and knew how to build with local materials. He had two beat-up trucks we could take over the reef, a high bulldozer with huge tires and a willing bulldozer driver. On top of all that, Taputuarai was the contractor who had been smart enough to figure out an economic way to extend the Faaa airport runway into the lagoon in order to bring jets into Tahiti. He was used to building both complicated and very simple projects. We got along well and a contract was signed without too much haggling. As I remember, it was for $100,000 for the runway, and I would be able to employ Taputuarai's crew to build the village buildings on an hourly basis.

The contract with Taputuarai did not include getting his equipment and materials to Tetiaroa. That was my responsibility, and I had to figure out how to get everything over the reef. First things first, and so I set out to find the right boat for the transport. I'd noticed that the public works boat in Papeete Harbor was an old military landing craft. Its bow opened, exposing a ramp that could be lowered onto a reef, making it easy to roll off our equipment. I went to see the person in charge of public works, and was told we could rent the boat for two days, providing the captain granted permission first. His name was Olivier, and it was he who would have to determine if unloading on the reef was feasible. I found out where Olivier lived, and Marlon, who had just returned from Paris shooting *Last Tango*, came with me. We called, but no one answered. We knocked against the door frame, and called out "Olivier, Olivier"... still no response. Marlon peeked in and there he was: a skinny, wizened old guy dressed only in his shorts, lying flat on his tummy in the middle of the floor, passed out. Marlon crept over to the counter, found a half-empty bottle of Scotch, placed it in Olivier's hand, and tip-toed back out. We left him there exactly as we'd found him.

Returning the next day, we found Olivier in good humor. An old salt with leathery skin, and still wearing his sun-bleached shorts, he told us he had been sailing the South Pacific all of his life and was about to retire. We explained our reef dilemma. He didn't like our idea one bit, but Marlon was able to charm him, and talked him into landing Taputuarai's bulldozer and trucks on the reef. Marlon's powers of persuasion cannot be underestimated. He was, after all, an extremely accomplished actor.

I took out a $3,000 insurance policy from Lloyds of London the next day.

About this time, my family was delighted to come down to Tahiti to be together for a few months. We lived in Punauuia with Marlon and Tarita. On weekends, Marlon, Zeke, I, and our families would hike up into the mountains looking for wild fruit. I remember our trips up the Punaruu Valley trails well. We'd hike up into the mountains amongst Tahitians carrying fruit down to town on poles resting on their shoulders, to be sold at the markets. The trails followed the Punaruu River, and every once in a while there would be a deep swimming hole. Our kids would climb onto overhanging branches and dive into the pools below, where curious, slithering fat eels as big as my thigh would tickle us. The fresh, cold water felt perfect after a sweaty hike over slippery jungle paths. Marlon would float on his back down the rapids carrying one of the kids on his big tummy. Sabrina counts that experience among her funniest and fondest memories — floating down the Punaruu on Marlon's belly.

During the rainy season, Tahiti's rugged mountain ranges and lush valleys create rushing rivers, spectacular waterfalls, and grottos. Many of the falls are hidden on the interior of the island, but some can be accessed from the main circle road; that is, if one is willing to scramble up roaring streams of water to the falls that descend into crystal-clear pools. These fresh water rivers and streams that gush through valleys into lagoons kill the coral in the surrounding reef. This is why reef passes can be found opposite valleys and rivers. Some passes have become so big that they allow good-sized vessels to maneuver through.

It was great fun coming upon these waterfalls, and I occasionally set out to explore Tahiti's valleys just to find them. In the dense jungle, they could be heard before being seen. All of a sudden, a clearing would appear and there, right before your eyes, were towering sheets of water hundreds of feet high, running over black volcanic rock. The babysitter, Michele, was good at locating and exploring falls, and was especially adept at maneuvering up the rocky riverbeds, shoeless and sure-footed. Once she led me to one of her favorite falls. I followed gingerly, sweating, slipping, sliding, and falling way behind, but eventually found her, standing in a clear transparent pool, under torrents of falling water, her drenched *pareu* around her hips, a lovely, svelte white figure against cold black volcanic rock, her long blond hair dripping wet. It was a sight to behold. While standing under the fall, I was astonished by the force of the water on my skin. It actually hurt. I was also mindful of falling rocks. Michele was much less concerned; the falling water "might pound some sense into me," she said.

I came to appreciate Tahiti's majestic, mysterious peaks even more than her shores. Some people had begun building houses high up in the mountains, seeking the glorious views and a cooler climate. Tea's mother had constructed a wonderful one-room, Japanese-style retreat on a fantastic site overlooking a 1,000-foot-deep gorge, half a dozen waterfalls, and the Pacific Ocean in the distance. Tetiaroa can be seen 33 miles away. Standing on the precipice and spotting that slight sliver of land on the horizon, Marlon once remarked, "Bernie, I can feel its magnetic pull in my gut."

On one occasion, Purea and her family gave a party there for Marlon, Alice, and me. Zeke, Tea, and her brother Johnny had baked pot brownies without telling anyone about the pot part. Everyone loved the brownies, including Alice, who didn't smoke, drink or do any drugs. Late that night, several cars left the party to return to Papeete. Marlon drove the first car, and I followed with Alice in the second. When we got down to the bottom of the mountain and onto the main road, Marlon's brake lights suddenly came on. He screeched to a stop, hesitated for a minute, and then proceeded around a large object blocking the road. As we approached the same spot, we saw a body lying in the middle of the road. Alice screamed, "Oh my God, Marlon's killed somebody!" She yelled, "Stop! Stop!" When we jumped out of the car, the body in the road was asleep, not dead. I tried to wake him, but couldn't budge him from his apparent drunken stupor. Zeke, Johnny, and I finally dragged the guy to the side of the road, got back in our cars, and laughed all the way home. The next morning Alice was still convinced that Marlon had killed someone. When we told her about the brownies, she got so angry that she wouldn't speak to any of us for several days.

Our three families took trips to Tetiaroa as well. Marlon would rent a boat, gather all of us, and off we would go for a camping weekend. We caught monstrous, bright-blue coconut crabs, 24 inches across from claw to claw. After building a fire on the beach, we threw them in the embers, and when they turned red, tossed them into the lagoon with a stick. We sat in the shallow water, and when the crabs hit and exploded, we ate the delicious morsels as they went floating by. Marlon, of course, tried to steal the biggest pieces, but the kids would fight him off, jumping on his back. It was great fun!

Having a meal with Marlon was always fascinating, whether at home, out with friends, or at a restaurant. While we ate together at his house in Punaauia, he would often comment on my table manners. "Bernie, why do you eat so delicately? Why do you sit up so straight? Why don't you shove the food in your mouth like me? Look, look what I'm doing," he'd say, as he crammed food into his mouth, slobbering all over the place. "Bernie, do it like me." I tried. I tried as hard as I could to shove piles of food in my mouth. I started laughing so hard that food fell out of my mouth. He was laughing too, screaming, "That's it! More, more." This went on a few minutes until I had to leave the table, clutching my stomach, laughing so hard. In a restaurant, Marlon would comment on other people's table manners too. He would distract me, steal food right off my plate; I'd look down, and he'd distract me again while he swiped another chunk. He was always stealing my food. I was usually amused, but at times ,embarrassed or dismayed. Table manners were not his strength.

One night in Los Angeles, Marlon came to dinner. He was there to meet my good friend, Alan Grinnell, his wife, Vee, and another couple. I thought they would get along famously, and they did. We had all had a good conversation before Dora brought out dinner and set it on the dining room table. Marlon reached across and grabbed both ends of the leg of lamb and, to the amazement of everyone at the table, started chomping on it. Dora and I were used to this kind of thing, but we worried about how our guests might perceive it. We were embarrassed, but relieved that they took it with aplomb.

I often wondered why Marlon pulled these childish stunts. I'm pretty sure that when among friends, he just wanted to get attention or a laugh. It was less clear why he'd "misbehave" among strangers. It may have been a form of control. Marlon needed to feel in control, I suppose, to mask his fear of being thought inadequate or stupid, or "found out." Marlon was extremely intelligent and perceptive, but he was also full of neuroses. I, like most who knew him well, let him get away with bad manners. I guess it added to his boyish charm. And besides, that's what friends do — accept each other for who we are. Others must have found him completely eccentric.

Marlon was fascinated by Alan, who is a physiologist who spoke that night with authority about science, the human brain, echo-locating bats, and even Mayan pottery. Marlon and he talked into the wee hours, and as Alan later told me, Marlon continued to telephone him for weeks after to ask him all kinds of questions. Marlon was immensely curious about all things scientific, and was good at absorbing information. His imagination, however, would

Top
Tarita and Agnes.

Bottom left
Tarita and Dora.

Bottom right
A flotilla.

Top
Guests arrive for a holiday weekend.

Bottom
Johnny and Moeata.

Top
Agnes and Tarita.

Bottom
A kaveo picnic.

Top
The island is crawling with coconut crabs (kaveos).

Bottom
Cooling off in the lagoon.

sometimes run wild. At one point, he told me he thought electric eels would be a good way to make electricity on Tetiaroa, so he bought some. I have no idea where one buys electric eels in L.A., but he kept them swimming around in an aquarium at his home on Mulholland Drive for a while. The tank was right off his bedroom, and every once in a while he'd go over and disturb the eels and try to monitor the electricity they would make. Alan told him he would need thousands of eels in the Tetiaroa lagoon to supply enough electricity to keep the lights on. One would have to figure out how to make them provide a constant current, and the eels would no doubt kill all the fish in the lagoon with their burst of electricity when annoyed. But once Marlon got an idea in his head, he would not let go. I'd listen to his schemes, wondering sometimes whether he was a genius or a madman.

Now that it looked like we were actually going to start building something on the island, Marlon started to invite his old friends from high school to the camp site. His sister Jocelyn also showed up, as well as some ex-girlfriends. They called him "Bud," his nickname as a teenager. After a while, I found myself calling him "Bud" as well, particularly when I, consciously or unconsciously, wanted to express my close rapport with him. I noticed on those occasions that Marlon liked to keep in touch with old friends, particularly old girlfriends. He helped them out whenever he could. His loyalty seemed boundless. Alice came along on these trips, and it was wonderful to see Marlon with his old chums and family, full of enthusiasm about his plans for the atoll.

On one such trip, we were all assembled at a long table on the beach. Marlon had invited a few of his scientist friends and their wives. They were conducting studies on how we might raise fish on the atoll in the future. This particular evening about twenty of us sat together in candlelight with lanterns set around us. I was between Alice and Reiko. The jungle beyond the table was not illuminated at all. As we were all eating and talking and having a good time, I caught a glimpse of a girl approaching the clearing. I remember thinking, "Someone must be coming back from the loo." Looking around the table, I realized that no one had been missing. Everyone was accounted for. So who was this girl? No one else seemed to notice her. No one was looking at her. She came closer and closer, and then just stood, gazing at us. It was then that I realized she was a *tupapa'u* who, for some reason, had appeared to me. She wore a white dress and a red flower behind her ear. I didn't dare say anything, particularly to Marlon, because he didn't like anyone talking about ghosts. The others might think I was nuts, or worse, get frightened. So I kept quiet. Ghosts were one of the few things Marlon seemed scared of, although he claimed he didn't believe in them. In fact, I heard him yelling one night: "Get away, get away, get away!" But there was no *tupapa'u*. He'd wrapped himself up in his mosquito netting.

I didn't want to disturb anyone at the table that night, so I simply watched the *tupapa'u* for a while as she kept on staring at us, smiling. After a while she just drifted away as quickly as she'd appeared. The next morning, Alice and I were the first ones up. We were drinking coffee silently until I couldn't bear it any more.

"Did you see anything funny last night?"

"Did you?" she responded, surprise in her voice.

"Did you see her?" I ventured carefully.

"Yes, I did." Alice spoke softly. "She wore a white dress and a red flower. You saw her, too?"

Alice and I never told anyone else about our apparition. We shared the bond of believers quietly, and laughed about it often.

I later found out the background story on that particular *tupapa'u*. Apparently, a long time ago, a Tahitian king had fallen in love with a young virgin and kidnapped her to Tetiaroa, but she wouldn't have anything to do with him and tried to escape. In frustration, the King warned her: "If you do not stay here with me, I will banish you to the coral head in the middle of the lagoon. You won't be able to get away, because the sharks will eat you. You'll remain there forever." She still refused his attention, so she was taken out to the coral and left there to die. To this day, Tahitians familiar with the story are afraid of her. Some have been known to fall in love with her. Legend has it that those who follow her into the lagoon never come back.

I had seen one *tupapa'u* before, in Marlon's house in Punaauia. I woke up in the dead of night, and standing there right in front of my bed appeared who I thought was Tarita, just looking at me. I closed and opened my eyes. "Tarita, is that you?" She just continued to stare at me. I figured out fast it wasn't Tarita, but a ghost also dressed in white, with a flower in her hair. She seemed to be floating above the floor. To my own surprise, I wasn't scared, just curious. She smiled at me, and I soon went back to sleep. When I told Tarita about it the next day, she said, "Don't tell Marlon. That *tupapa'u* has been around since before he bought the house from Omer Darr. (The same Omer Darr who owned the Fairweather). "No one knows who she is," she said, "Omer didn't tell Marlon that the house was haunted. He would never have bought it if he had been warned".

I continued to stay at Marlon's in Punaauia throughout the entire contractor bidding process. One of many things I discovered was that he liked to fix things. He was what the French refer to as a *bricoler*, a guy who likes to do it himself. He was particularly entranced with toilets. He was always working on the toilets in his house. I would find him with his rump up and his head behind the bowl at least once a week. He never seemed to get it quite right. He told me that he had fixed Tennessee Williams' toilet the first time he ever met him, which was in 1947 while working on the Broadway play *A Streetcar Named Desire*. I wondered if Mr. Williams had to call a plumber to repair Marlon's work.

I had ordered special low-flush toilets to be used in the village at Tetiaroa through the Whole Earth Catalogue. They were not commercially available at the time. They were made of plastic and looked a little weird, but they would save us a lot of water. When I told Marlon about them, he was very enthusiastic and wanted to try one out. I'd ordered twenty and had one delivered to his house in Punaauia. Unfortunately, the seats on these particular toilets were very small, and he overhung his prototype to a considerable degree. "We can't have people overhanging toilets like this. Get rid of them." It turned out it was too late to cancel the order, so they were shipped anyway, but never installed. I suspect there are twenty boxes of toilets lying in some storage shed on Tetiaroa even now.

Marlon wasn't the only one who liked to repair things. He had a Boston Whaler flat-bottomed boat that he'd used several times to get over the reef in Tetiaroa. It had big holes in the bottom of the hull, and he asked me if I would fix it for him. So I got the epoxy glue, foam, and fiberglass cloth from downtown Papeete, and brought everything up to the driveway where the boat was stored. One day, I was working barefoot in my bathing suit. The gluing, foaming, and sanding process left me with shavings and sticky fiberglass dust all over my body. In order to keep the mess out of my hair, I swiped a pair of Tarita's panties off the clothesline and put them on my head. When she drove up and saw me covered with dust, with her undies on my head, she screamed at the top of her lungs, "How dare you touch my underwear!" Just then a policeman drove up in his Jeep. The cop turned to Tarita and asked, "Do you want me to take him down to the station like this?" I was worried there for a moment, but it turned out the cop was Tarita's brother dropping in for a visit. Boy did I feel embarrassed! It took awhile for me to get it, and from that time on, I made sure I found something else to cover my head.

Marlon was a great observer. He was fascinated by small details, and would focus on them while committing the information to memory. Sometimes he became so lost in a detail, it seemed as if he were in a trance. One day, we were sitting across from each other and he noticed that one of my flip-flop soles was flapping in the breeze. "Bernie," he said, "how can you walk around like that? Gimme that shoe; I'll fix it." He grabbed my sandal, disappeared for five minutes, and came back with it glued back together. He had a need to control every little thing around him, even someone's footwear. Every detail had to be just right, in his personal life as well as with his acting. Sometimes this was not an easy thing to live with, but I, like most everyone else around him, got used to it.

Another time, as I walked through the living room, I discovered Marlon sitting on the couch crying really hard. He was obviously distraught, and I said, "Marlon, my God, what's happened?" He looked up and moaned, "I just lost my wife." I was shocked. "Marlon, what are you talking about?" But he just went on crying and whimpering, "I just lost my wife." I didn't know what to do for him. I was mystified and horrified that Tarita might be dead, but I couldn't think of what to say, and I didn't want to interfere, so trying to think straight, I crept away and left him alone. I went into my room and sat on my bed, bewildered. A few moments later, after he had composed himself, he came to me and said, "Bernie, I have to go to Paris tomorrow. I'm doing a film with Bertolucci. Will you take me to the airport at the crack of dawn?" Much relieved, I understood right away that Tarita was fine, and that Marlon had been preparing for a scene. Yes, every detail mattered to him, particularly when it came to acting.

The following morning, he came into my room very early to wake me. It was still dark, so he turned on a light. We were both naked. Everyone sleeps nude in the tropics. There was a full-length mirror on one of the closet doors in front of us, and as I got up out of bed rubbing my eyes, Marlon said, "Bernie, for the next two weeks, I'd love to have your body - my head, but your body." He was going to shoot *Tango*, and he was a little embarrassed about his big tummy. Neither of us knew it at the time, but the scene he had rehearsed the night before would make cinematic history.

One of the last things we did after having the airstrip plans approved by the authorities was to set up communications between Tetiaroa and Tahiti. I had brought a short-wave radio set down from Los Angeles and asked Tea's brother Johnny, who knew all about radios, to come out and help set it up with an antennae system pointed toward Tahiti. Naturally, this called for an expedition including Zeke, Tea, Johnny, his girlfriend Moeata, Michele Darr, and as many others as we could bring along for a fun weekend. Getting the 50-foot-long antennae wires aimed in the right direction turned out to be the big trick. Luckily, Johnny climbed coconut trees like a monkey, and he had to climb at least a dozen before we were finally able to reach Radio Mahina, the central radio tower for all of the islands.

Ours was the type of radio communication that needs shouting "over" between sender and receiver, as in: "Hello, can you hear me? Over." And the response: "I hear you. What's up? Over." The operator at Mahina would patch the call through to the regular telephone system. Pretty soon Tea became our communication manager on Tahiti. If anything was needed, or we had some kind of emergency, we would contact Radio Mahina. "This is Tetiaroa. Over." They'd say: "Who do you want to talk to? Over." They'd connect us to Tea, who'd scream, "Bernie, how are things? Over." I'd yell back: "Just great. We need batteries, a saw, canvas, rum... Over." This was how we communicated for the next two years. I still tend to shout on the telephone. During construction, we used the system for ordering parts, food, and supplies, or to get assistance. We also spoke with Marlon wherever he was in the world at the time, in order to keep him up to date on our progress. It was a rudimentary communication system, but it worked like a charm for us. The only challenge was that Radio Mahina had open airwaves, so everyone could, and would, listen in on everyone else. We couldn't talk about secrets, and we had to be very careful of what we said about whom, and to whom. Everyone listening to Radio Mahina for, let's say, the weather, could also hear me talking to Tea, or Tea talking to Marlon. He did not ever want reporters to find out where he was, so we developed a code. Marlon was "Octopus." "Coconuts are falling" meant that Tarita was coming out to the island. Or if someone was scheduling a tryst, they might say: "The supply boat arrives at sunset." There were curiously inventive conversations going on at times, some of them clearly due to the agreement Marlon had evidently reached with Tarita. No hanky panky when they were together, but when they were apart, it was a different story. He kept his part of the bargain by making sure he had no "visitors" while she was on Tetiaroa, and she didn't go to the bars on the waterfront when he was in Tahiti. Though they lived together and stayed together for the rest of his life, and Marlon always took care of her and their children, they never got married.

Johnny looking on as I try out our radio.

Our camp site on Onetahi. The old copra drying shed in foreground with drinking water drum under the gutter of the shed. My tent in background.

LANDING ON THE REEF

The Underwater Bulldozer
Building an Airstrip

Finally, the day arrived for our cargo boat, Meherio, to disembark on the reef. It was March 18, 1972. I had consulted the weather bureau for the best time of year for high tides, low winds, and small swells. Marlon was back in Paris working, and his good old friend Gaston, who had a small movie studio in Punaauia, was to film the operation. (He also provided porno movies for the ship's crew.) Insurance company representatives were to be onboard the Meherio, as I had purchased the $3,000 worth of insurance for that day alone. Purea and her maid had come along to observe from the beach while sipping champagne.

Everyone understood that this disembarkation could be dangerous. The Meherio had arrived the day before the landing, carrying the makings of a raft upon which to float the truck, equipment, and bulldozer from the reef across the lagoon onto shore. The raft, made of 2 x 12 planks and 50-gallon drums, would be unloaded at sea and taken over the reef by swimmers. The raft itself was to be constructed overnight in the lagoon, and had to be ready for use at 7:00 a.m. on the big day.

Agnes and I were sitting on the remnants of the pier off Motu Rimatuu on a beautiful and clear afternoon, when off in the distance we finally spotted the Meherio. She was chock full of workmen and three months worth of everything we needed to build the airstrip. We, the advance party, had arrived before to set up communications and to check on the weather, tides, and waves. I had sent back a message via ship to shore radio that the conditions were perfect and we were ready to go. In spite of all precautions, there had been a last-minute delay brought on by unforeseen weather in Tahiti and poor communication between Tetiaroa and Papeete. The additional wait had affected my mood and I had been growing gloomy as the hours wore on.

I had been working toward this day for months, and what I wanted most at that moment was a cold beer. When I saw the Meherio approaching at last, I waved, shouted, and laughed, barely believing my eyes. There it was! Finally, something concrete was going to happen after nearly a year of postponements, negotiations, disappointments, and frustrations that more often than not left me feeling drained. The negative attitude we had run across everywhere had left its effect on me. I was getting tired of hearing "You're dreamers. This can't be done on a shoe string." The fact that I had to attend to every detail personally, and the sometimes lackadaisical attitude of the Tahitians with their "*aita, pea pea*" attitude, assuming with no reason that "everything is OK, no problem, not to worry," — something I had found so charming at first — had gotten to me. I was growing impatient. I needed things to work out now.

The Meherio was truly a sight for sore eyes, and as she drew nearer, I could make out our contractor, Taputuarai: short and stout, dressed in a yellow windbreaker, waving madly and grinning from ear to ear. There was 80-year-old Gaston with his movie camera, dressed all in white, looking like a scarecrow in his funny straw hat. And our drunken friend Captain Olivier was springing all about like a monkey, shouting orders. I am sure he was not at all pleased about bringing his boat so close to the reef, not to mention about possibly risking his so far unblemished reputation as a sea captain.

The decision about where to land was crucial, and had to be made at the last moment depending on specific wind and surf conditions on the reef. During the early morning, the west side of the reef had been relatively calm. But by mid-afternoon, things had changed. The wind had shifted and the sea was high and choppy, with a 6-foot surf pounding the reef. I took the zodiac, met the Meherio 50 yards out, and took aboard Taputuarai and Olivier. We had to find a site to unload, and fast. Olivier looked really concerned when Taputuarai demanded: "Just put me on the reef anywhere. I'll figure out how to get ashore from there." We identified a portion of the reef that was concave and formed a shallow bay. I had previously picked out a couple of areas along this bay that looked promising. We located one spot in particular, close to the reef, where we could at least unload the materials needed to construct our homemade pontoon raft. Later, after getting those materials off, we would look for a landing site to unload the big bulldozer and the rest of the supplies. Taputuarai was relieved. He and his men could get to work. It was nearly 5:00 in the afternoon by now, and we only had a couple more hours of sunlight. We raced back to the Meherio, which was making slow and elegant circles in the middle of the deep blue ocean, waiting for us to tell them where to unload the raft material in the water.

There was frantic activity aboard: sailors were undoing whaleboats and unfastening empty 50-gallon drums and the lumber to be used to construct the raft. Olivier was jumping around flailing his arms, barking orders, very much in command–of what, I'm not sure, as no one appeared to be paying any attention. Gaston was filming the whole episode for Marlon, and once on board, I finally got my ice-cold beer.

Before I knew it, two whale boats were being lowered into the water, one with bundles of 2" x 12" planks, and the other with the empty drums. The first boat set off towards the reef. The oars were in pulling position to take the boat to the top of the frothy white surf, and then they were pushing back in order to avoid hitting the coral reef. It was a spectacular sight. The men tossed the wood bundles out into the waves, and swimmers, who were waiting in the swells, then guided the bundles onto the reef. The wood bounced all over the reef like so many matchsticks. On the reef, more men gathered the flying wood and pushed it into the lagoon. It's a wonder no one was killed.

The second whale boat overturned heading in, and everything momentarily disappeared into the foam until out popped a head here, a head there. All of the men knew exactly how to react: to dive back out to sea, not fight the top of the wave, find the middle section, and swim away hard. They knew not to hang on to anything beneath the waves, to come up for air, dive back under, and continue swimming away. After each of the men emerged from the ocean side of the reef, and each knew the others were okay, there were great shouts of laughter all around. The men recuperated the capsized whale boat, swam after and collected the drums, and pushed them back towards the reef. The swimmers then maneuvered the drums to the point where the waves were breaking, and over they toppled, topsy-turvy in the air, splashing down into the lagoon side like ping-pong balls. Those waiting in the lagoon captured their "prey," and slung the drums together, while regularly falling into the shallow lagoon screaming with laughter. It seemed that they were all enjoying themselves immensely! I was a nervous wreck.

Luckily, it turned out to be a clear moonlit night. One group was able to work in the lagoon constructing the raft, while another placed the empty drums under the raft for buoyancy. The raft would have to carry 12 tons of equipment. The big trick would be to hold the raft in place as it was being loaded. Of course, one of the men had been delegated to go spear fishing for the evening meal.

Captain Olivier wondering if this is as crazy as it looks.

I left the Meherio and its captain with a bottle of Scotch, and along with Taputuarai, raced toward the reef on the Zodiac. Catching a wave, we rode across the lagoon to where beloved Agnes was waiting for us with rum punches. It was a marvelous treat. We all gathered around a huge campfire on the beach that night to enjoy the catch of the day: clams, lobster, and raw fish. Everyone was weary, but content.

Captain Olivier's work was done for the day, and he was glad he didn't have to maneuver his ship too close to the reef. He had gotten away unscathed for now. We had decided on a location for disembarkation the following morning, where the reef was solid and had a good, deep slope that didn't allow for a large wave build-up. The bottom wasn't too deep for the captain to drop anchor, and there weren't too many coral heads inside the lagoon, so we could easily navigate the raft. We were in this together, and there was good fellowship all around. The landing would take place at 6:00 the next morning. Olivier had decided to return to Papeete overnight. I didn't like the idea, but he was the captain, and made his own decisions regarding his craft. As it turned out, I was right to have been concerned. When we arose at dawn, the Meherio had not returned. Everyone was sure that the captain had gotten drunk ashore.

I tried to keep this latest delay in stride. There was an awful lot to keep us busy while we were waiting. It took all morning to create a pass for the raft that would allow it to get from the landing site on the reef through the coral heads in the lagoon all the way to shore. We had no proper tools, just pieces of wood, steel pipe, and a couple of large logs to use as crowbars and levers. At 2:30 that afternoon, the Meherio appeared on the horizon, and everyone's face lit up. This was it. The great bulldozer-on-the-reef gambit was about to begin.

The captain's hangover must have been superb, and as I watched him make one dry run sounding the bottom, and then make a big turn, I was sure that the bastard was chickening out and running back home. But he turned again and in he came, creating terrific excitement. People were running on the reef trying to get into position, tripping over themselves, as the Meherio bore in, bow doors now wide open. Up, up, and in she came–scrape, squeak, crumble, splash, and crash onto the reef. First out came the dump truck loaded with food, gear, and beer. Then sailors rolled drums filled with fuel out onto the reef. And finally, the bulldozer came roaring out, like a caged animal being unleashed.

Men were carrying equipment off the boat onto the reef and onto the raft. I was falling all over myself taking photos. Taputuarai stationed himself in the middle of it all shouting instructions. Olivier, red-eyed, up on the bridge, crouched over the tube to the engine room ready to order: "Back off!" The waves crashed. The steel bow door thudded as it was lifted and slammed back down again by the surf. The bulldozer, carrying equipment back and forth from the ship onto the reef, was forcing her back out to sea. The Meherio's motors made a terrible rumble, throwing up foam as the captain drove her farther up against the reef to make the unloading possible.

Unloading planks to make a raft.

Empty drums for the raft are taken to the reef.

Top
Next morning —the raft made overnight is waiting for the Meherio to return.

Bottom
Someone always goes fishing.

At one point, only the front wheels of the dump truck made it onto the raft, forcing the opposite side up into the air. The rear wheels settled into the lagoon, and the drums simply floated away. It took at least an hour to remedy the whole mess. There was stuff all over the reef: 50-gallon drums of diesel fuel, boxes, boat motors, pumps, an 8.5 kilowatt Lister generator, crates filled with food. Finally the Meherio was completely unloaded, her bow door shut as she backed off the reef, luckily unharmed, and her very happy captain waved *nana*, goodbye. The cargo was left in 6 inches of water, resting on a reef in the middle of the South Pacific, and still half a mile out from Motu Onetahi in the lagoon of Tetiaroa, which itself is near nothing at all! But the trickiest and perhaps most dangerous part of the maneuver was over. That day will be etched in my memory forever.

We worked that night until we could work no longer. When we stopped, the only pieces of equipment remaining on the reef were the bulldozer and the generator, which had been raised up out of the water and left resting on 50-gallon drums. We were too tired to eat and just fell asleep.

I was awakened that night by the ferocious whacking sound of the flaps on my canvas tent, and I knew we might be in big trouble. Sometimes squalls and wild winds came rushing through and ended as quickly as they'd begun. Other times they lasted for days on end. Luckily, that particular night, the winds subsided within a few hours and I fell back into a deep sleep. As I looked out of my tent early the next morning, I realized, much to my dismay, that the raft we had moored along the beach was no longer there. Others, already awake, were on the beach. We quickly discovered pieces of the raft, as well as several of the flotation drums strewn across the sand, and in some cases blown into the vegetation behind our camp. I ran to collect my binoculars and, staring through them, found that the bulldozer was still where we had left it, but that the generator had disappeared during the storm. The bulldozer driver and I rushed out to the reef by Zodiac, only to find absolutely no trace of the generator, or its crate. Our only source of electricity was lost. If the bulldozer didn't start, building the runway would have to be put off, and the disembarkation would have been for nothing. I was numb with anguish, wondering why I had left the generator and the bulldozer out there overnight. The skies had fooled me. I should have pushed and screamed and yelled at Taputuarai to work throughout the night.

The driver ran across the reef, climbed up onto his bulldozer, turned on the ignition, and amazingly, it started right up. What a huge relief! He knew that without a raft, he had to chance driving the thing right through the lagoon. We prayed the water wasn't too deep. Slowly, he set off, and just as slowly, he sank into the water until the 6-foot-high tires were completely submerged, followed by the engine, and finally, the driver himself. All I could still see from my vantage point on the reef was the bulldozer's vertical diesel tail pipe extension and the driver's white cap skimming along the top of the water. After a few heart thumping minutes, I was ecstatic to see the driver's head emerge, and then his body! He had been holding his breath underwater, and now he continued traversing the lagoon, smiling from ear to ear until he reached the shore one half mile away. In spite of my joy, looking at the tire tracks on the virgin sand, I couldn't help asking myself: "Is this the beginning–or the beginning of the end?"

There was a huge amount of work to do. It took a week to get everything in order before we could actually start working on the airstrip. First off, we had to have fresh water. A dormitory had to be built for the workers, and all the equipment that had been submerged in salt water had to be cleaned right away so it wouldn't corrode. Sanitation facilities had to be constructed asap. Taputuarai and his crew set up their housing and office, made of plywood with a tin roof, next to our survey crew's original campsite from the year before. The bulldozer scraped out a large ditch for bathing, and we dug a well for drinking water. It took awhile for the water to clear in the ditch and the well, and in the meantime we bathed in the lagoon. The old 50-gallon drum at the campsite had refilled with rainwater, and we were drinking that, even though it had a bit of a rusty taste. I had brought along biodegradable soap made without chemicals, but the Tahitians were using their own coconut oil soap. I had not given my lecture to the crew, and I knew that in time, Marlon and I would have to establish some rules about soaps and detergents, motor oils, and insecticides in our effort to preserve the atoll ecology. But in that first week, I didn't want to say anything to Taputuarai; it was too early in our working relationship. We rigged up a shower by bracketing a 50-gallon drum to a tree. The drum was filled one pail at a time with fresh, cool water from the well, and, believe me, it was heaven to be able to wash the salt and sweat off our skin. I had left my tent from my previous trip, and Agnes and I made use of the existing shacks we had found on the survey trip. We cooked in the old kitchen hut, and I used the other shanty as an office and radio shack. The Tahitians cooked over an open fire pit right next door, and shared their food with Agnes and me. Our little group totaled about two dozen. Work began at 8:00 a.m., stopped at noon for an hour or so, and then again at 3:00 p.m., when everyone went fishing. Sometimes we went looking for lobster by moonlight on the reef. We took off weekends, when, again, everyone went fishing. It was the beginning of a good 18 months of construction work. I was elated and apprehensive at the same time. After all, I had very little practical knowledge of life in the South Seas. I would have to learn as I went along.

Initially, the extent of sanitation on the atoll was a shovel and a hole in the woods, or maybe a trip to the lagoon. Believe it or not, I preferred the latter, since it was convenient to just jump in the water and not worry about remembering to bring toilet paper or digging a

Top
The Meherio arrives. Onetahi in the background.

Bottom
Unloading the Meherio on the reef.

Top
*Attempting to load the
truck on the raft.*

Bottom
*Success!
Taputuarai is in the yellow slicker.*

Top
*Enough fuel and materials on the
raft for three months.*

Bottom
*The Meherio leaves, and
we are stranded on the reef.*

Top
One happy man. He did the impossible, driving his bulldozer through the lagoon while holding his breath underwater.

Bottom
The bulldozer carrying all that was left on the raft.

Was this the beginning, or the beginning of the end?

hole. It did take some adjusting: I had to get accustomed to squatting in the lagoon where curious fish swam around and seemed to enjoy nibbling at my bottom. I got used to it though, and even thought to myself that I could get hooked on these nibbling fish. As soon as we possibly could, we built plated coconut leaf privies over cement block septic tanks. Keeping contaminants, particularly spilled diesel fuel and cleaning fluids, away from the fresh water lens would remain a perennial problem. There was a constant danger of affecting the fresh water lens, because it lay only 2 feet below the surface.

Taputuarai had brought two 25-foot outrigger canoes with him. Fitted with outboard motors, they were useful in hauling material around the lagoon, as well as in transporting both provisions and visitors from the old wharf at Motu Rimatuu, which remained our point of contact for the supply boat that came by whenever it could. Tea would call in on the radio from her house in Punaauia at 10 a.m. each morning to ask how things were going, and to arrange for the boat to make deliveries from Tahiti, weather permitting.

We tried making concrete blocks ourselves out of the plentiful coral sand mixed with some cement, but they were too porous. I asked our good skipper, Olivier, to bring a load of high-strength concrete block from Papeete. It took a couple of weeks for him to be able to do it, but one fine day our beloved Meherio appeared outside the reef. The problem was, this time it was a Sunday and everyone was off fishing or sleeping. I couldn't get a work party together. Olivier didn't want to wait overnight, and I remembered what Gooding had told me about getting things done in Tahiti: "If you want things done, do them yourself." So I paddled a canoe out to the reef, and, believe it or not, I spent the entire day unloading 800 concrete blocks onto the reef myself. Years later, when I was making an application for residency in French Polynesia, my fingerprints had to be verified by the FBI, and their report came back: "No prints on this man's fingers." I wasn't surprised; the concrete blocks had worn them off!

A supply boat returned periodically. Whenever we spotted it outside the reef by the old copra wharf, everyone went out to greet it excitedly. If the surf was not too big, we could unload; otherwise, the boat would depart with our supplies, and we would have to wait for better conditions. I was learning that schedules in Tahiti could not be counted on. Nature too often had different plans. Agnes, Taputuarai and the majority of the crew were supposed to leave on the supply boat once they had completed their work. As it happened, Dora and Sabrina arrived on the same boat that took Taputuarai and his crew back to Tahiti. After unloading some supplies, among them fresh baguettes and beer, Agnes, Taputuarai, and his crew bid us farewell and returned to Tahiti. All that remained on the atoll that afternoon were my small family, and seven Tahitians accompanied by a bulldozer and a decrepit old truck. That would be it for many months, except for occasional visits by Taputuarai, Marlon, and members of his family. These seven men, their machines, and I would build the airstrip.

Things changed right way. While Agnes and I had been living with Taputuarai and his men, we all ate together as a group. But as soon as Dora and Sabrina arrived, the Tahitians left us alone at meal times. I was sad because I had really enjoyed the company of the Tahitians. After a short while, they realized that we were not exactly award-winning fishermen. Sabrina, Dora, and I used gill nets that had relatively large holes in the netting, allowing smaller fish to swim through and trapping the larger by the gills. We attached the net to two sticks in the lagoon at night and every morning would find that we'd caught half a dozen mullet. After a while, we were growing pretty tired of eating the same thing every day. Tonio, one of the workers Dora was particularly fond of, took pity on us and would often drop off some of his own catch. When he noticed that none of my family really knew how to clean fish properly, he taught us how to scale and gut using a sharp shell. He also showed us how to wash the dishes in the lagoon with sand. It was not the most sanitary practice in the world, but it did save on soap, and it fed the little fish that ate the scraps. We had to constantly make sure we were not leaving food remains lying around our camp, in particular fish and fish scales, as they'd attract flies and mosquitoes. Camping made the notion of protecting the environment even more of a challenge, for other than the campfire, we didn't yet have any proper disposal methods in place. We were learning how to live gently on our little island home, and we absolutely loved it. Most of the time.

Every once in a while, Dora grew weary of being chief-cook-and-bottle-washer, as well as camp-cleaner-upper. Spotting a passing fishing boat one morning, she swam to the reef, stood up on the reef, took off her top, and waved them in. She hitched a ride to Papeete, phoned Tea, borrowed her credit card, a dress and shoes, and flew to Los Angeles on the first flight out.

"Where's Mommy?" Sabrina asked at dinnertime.
"I don't know, maybe she's still fishing."

Then Tea called to tell us the news. She said that she would be thrilled to come out and be happy to take care of Sabrina, but she had her own kids to take care of.

We had dinner with the crew that night. They had a lot of fun teasing me about my wife who had escaped, flown the coop. Sabrina and I got a kick out of it too. That was Dora! She came back about a week later.

Our little campsite was just a stone's throw from where the Tahitian workers lived, along with their equipment, drums of fuel, trucks, and the bulldozer. We had our tent, the kitchen hut, the "office" hut, a shower, and a privy. The supply boat that brought Dora back after her escape also brought us a little kerosene refrigerator, a stove run on bottled gas, and a "garde manger," a screened-in stand-up storage unit for bread and leftovers. It worked well for keeping out the flies, geckos, and ever-present rats. That marvelous little kitchen kept us going for almost two years. I would spend the day in the field with my surveying equipment plotting the airstrip, or working in the office hut on architectural drawings. One day, while setting up and leveling my surveyor's tripod, I had a flashback to my early childhood. I had been looking then at a *National Geographic* and a photo of a surveyor in the jungle of some faraway country. He was wearing khaki shorts and was shirtless, surrounded by vines and workers hacking away at the foliage. I remember wishing to someday be like this man. And here I was, 30 years later, doing the same thing! I wondered if one subconsciously pushes oneself into situations that validate childhood dreams.

Sabrina had the run of the *motu*. Dora home-schooled her near the beach under some shade trees. The rest of their time they spent swimming, fishing, sketching, reading, or figuring out how to cook the catch of the day. We ate only what was available on the island or from the lagoon, and we ate well: coconut, hearts of palm, all kinds of delicious fresh fish, lobster from the reef, crab, and when the boat came from Papeete, fresh lettuce, watermelons, baguettes, yams, taro, and pineapple. We had to cut down over 1,000 coconut trees to build the airstrip, and if I had had my wits about me, I would have sent hearts of palm to the market in Papeete, where they were selling for $5 a piece. I noticed that the workers sent them home to their families, which must have been a real treat for them. The crew knew a good deal when they saw one!

It was after a couple of months, during one of our very pleasant noontime meals on the beach, that literally out of the blue, a huge Pan Am 747 swooped down a couple of hundred feet (it felt like ten) above the lagoon and then flew off. "Gotta be Marlon," I said. Sure enough, he showed up the next day to see how everything was going. In those days, Pan Am pilots were old timers who had been flying in Polynesia since World War II. They were unorthodox "cowboys," always ready to give their passengers the thrill of a lifetime. I can only imagine what would happen to a commercial pilot who tried that kind of stunt today. Sometime in the 1930s, Pan Am pioneered aviation over the Pacific using amphibious Clipper ships, puddle jumpers outfitted with sleeping compartments. The planes would island hop, dropping into a lagoon if a runway wasn't available. We got to know some of those pilots. I still miss those guys and their crews.

A month later, Marlon returned with Tarita and Teihotu. He also had Christian and Miko in tow, his sons from a previous marriage, and his old friend Reiko, who would take care of the kids. Marlon was pleased with the progress we had made. The trees and brush had been cut down at the airstrip site; we had started to cut the trunks of the coconut trees into logs, and for the first time, we could see across the island from lagoon to lagoon.

Unlike Marlon, Tarita loved to fish. She had adored fishing with her father as a child on Bora Bora. He taught her all the tricks one can use with a hand line (that is, without a pole), where fish hide in coral, where to search for certain kinds of fish, which are the tastiest, just when to tug on the line, and what kind of bait to use depending on the kind of fish you wish to catch. Tarita would head out by herself in a canoe early in the morning. She looked beautiful: dark-skinned, slim, and elegant in her red bikini, her hair wrapped beneath her big straw hat. She'd stay out for hours and return with plenty of fish for everybody. She would spread out her catch and line it up on the beach, next to the rippling waters of the lagoon, for all to admire. The snub-nosed, buck-toothed parrot fish with their rainbow-colored scales were my favorite to look at, but not to eat. They had too many fine bones. I found the black surgeonfish the tastiest. Tarita showed Reiko how to clean, gut, and scale, and both Reiko and Dora how to avoid being cut removing the surgeonfish scales, which were tough and spiked. They also learned how to make *poisson cru*, those scrumptious chunks of raw fish, marinated in lime juice and coconut milk, and served cold.

The diminutive and lovely Reiko, when not looking after the kids, would wear her *pareu* low around her waist, her ample breasts bare, and her long braided hair dangling down her back under her floppy hat. Dora wore Bermuda shorts and a halter, and Tarita her red bikini. The women made a disparate but lovely trio sitting at the water's edge. Watching them from afar, Marlon and I remarked how Gauguin would have liked to sketch them. Marlon wandered around in a *pareu* or baggy shorts, an oversized shirt, and an old, ripped straw hat cocked on the side of his head. Tetiaroa was the one place in the world where Marlon could, and would, completely drop out and disengage.

Dora and I had made great strides in the old kitchen hut. We left it open on two sides and kept the sand floor. I had made stools, shelves, and a table out of driftwood. Both the refrigerator and the garde manger sat on legs set in tin cans filled with kerosene to keep the ants out. We spent a lot of energy fending off rodents, crabs, and other pests who had their sights set on our food. After a while, we just got used to them and shooed them away.

All of us *popaas* ate together at a long outdoor table, also made of driftwood. The wood was gray and velvety to the touch from years of exposure to sun and sea. We sat next to each other on long benches in the shade, and ate off of enameled tin plates Tea had sent us from a Chinese store in Papeete. The plates were decorated with Chinese floral designs, and I thought that they would be perfect for our future hotel dining room. Like the Tahitians, we ate mostly with our fingers, and scurried to the lagoon to wash them off when absolutely necessary. In the evenings, we dined by the light of old-fashioned, beautifully hand-painted, glass kerosene lamps that Tea had discovered in a tiny shop in Papeete. We tried and tried to find more for the future hotel rooms, but it seemed that Tea had gotten the few that were left in Tahiti.

After dinner Marlon would sometimes disappear down by the lagoon, where he might fall asleep under the stars, only to wake up at dawn, cold and stiff and mosquito-bitten. We'd see him straggle down the beach at dawn and into his tent, where he would sleep until noon.

He and I might meet in the afternoon, and he would tell me how much he loved being on the island, how much he cherished "the calm, the solitude, the freedom," and say that he wanted so much to live "in harmony with this little piece of the universe." And then he'd add: "But Bernie, see what you can do to get rid of the fucking mosquitoes!"

Other times Marlon would stay up late with us and tell stories by the light of the flickering kerosene lamps. He was a fantastic raconteur and adored an audience. One night Dora remarked that she was curious as to why Marlon, having been such a huge success on the stage in New York in the late 1940s, had come to Hollywood to pursue a career in film, even though he seemed not to enjoy it. He didn't answer, and I knew he didn't like the question. His face contorted, and in the silence, I wondered whether he'd be annoyed and leave the table in disgust. Instead he came back from his reverie to explain that he'd been living penniless in France when the producer Stanley Kramer sent him a ticket back to the States. Kramer had asked him to consider making a film called *The Men*. Marlon wasn't interested in doing movies, but he told us "the money was good." He didn't appear to want to discuss it any further, and veered off the subject to describe instead his arrival at a movie studio in Los Angeles in 1949. He told us he didn't know a soul in Hollywood at the time, and that someone or other had been assigned to take him around and introduce him to the studio head. Marlon told us that he'd been alerted that this fellow was extremely sensitive about the size of his nose. He had been instructed that whatever he did, not to look at the guy's nose. Breaking into hysterics, Marlon proceeded to describe how he had entered the man's office in terror of offending him, offered his hand and, uncontrollably gaping in amazement at his face, had said, " Glad to meet you, Mr. Nose!"

Our *popaa* campsite had grown quite a bit, when the Tahitian workers decided to move to the other side of the island. The idea of separating into groups of Tahitians and non-Tahitians was exactly what Marlon and I didn't want to happen, but it became a delicate problem that we never quite overcame, let alone truly understood. We discussed at length how the master planning process for Tetiaroa had to be more fluid in response to cultural and social realities. We simply had to react to how people obviously wished to live there, as opposed to how we thought they ought to live.

When Marlon and Tarita went back to Papeete, they left Teihotu, Christian, Miko, and Reiko with us. Now there were more tents, more kids, more people to feed. Sabrina was seven, Teihotu was nine, and Miko eleven; they pretty much looked after themselves playing on the beach, swimming, chasing, and terrorizing each other. Twelve-year-old Christian was another matter.

Top
Tea doing the dishes in the lagoon.

Bottom
Dora learns how to scale a fish with a shell.

Top
Our kitchen hut.

Bottom left
The good life, lobster and kaveo.

Bottom right
Reiko weaves coconut fronds.

Top left
Drying out our tent after a storm.

Top right
Decorations from land and sea.

Bottom
Dora serving lunch.

Top
Sabrina.

Bottom
Sabrina and me.

He needed constant supervision and Reiko had her hands full. Christian loved to throw machetes at trees, missing most of the time. When he did hit a tree, the machete would often bounce off, flying into space. Our peaceful existence had changed, and I must admit, Dora and I felt invaded.

We were building the airstrip while saving as many local building materials as we could. The coconut tree provided woven *niau* made from its leaves, posts and planks from its trunk. The root balls, when dug out, went into a compost heap together with all the brush we cut down. Small trees or branches were saved for use as rafters, and the two ironwood trees in the path of the runway were saved to be sawed later into planks for the bar top and tabletops in the dining room. I had learned from Paul Faugerat that coconut wood is extremely hard, except for its mid-section. It would make good lumber. I needed a way to saw the trunks into planks, and located an Alaskan Sawmill machine in the ever-trusty, dog-eared Whole Earth Catalogue that followed me everywhere I went. Marlon was enthusiastic about a new machine to play with, and immediately ordered one to be sent to us. We made planks and joists, but they were not wider than 6 inches. Larger sizes could not be made, as each log had to be quarter-cut to avoid the mid-section. Cupping, we found, would occur as the sapwood in the center dried out. Eventually, we set up a sawmill operation that produced beautiful, smooth, honey-colored floorboards.

Following the Tahitian tradition of construction, the leaves and coconut logs were bundled separately, dried for a month, and then put in the lagoon to soak up salt water, which acted as a preservative. This was another effort to keep chemicals off the atoll. After the landing strip had been completely cleared, the bulldozer carefully scraped away the small amount of topsoil above the sand, and stockpiled it to be used later, when we would plant grass. The root balls had to be taken out of the ground, as they would have rotted and made holes in the runway. My training with the Sea Bees in the 1950s had not been wasted; I knew something about building runways. In fact, early in the Tetiaroa planning process, I visited Port Hueneme, California, my old Sea Bee base. I talked to veterans of World War II, guys who had actually built runways on coral in the South Pacific. I picked up some practical advice. "Grass?" they said. "Forget it." I should have listened to them. I didn't. Our Tetiaroa airstrip was to have a grass surface with borders of white sand so it could be seen at night, as I had made no provision for lighting the runway in order to save energy. The entire process of clearing, grading, sifting and replacing the soil, and compacting and planting the runway was to have taken three months according to the contract, but it actually took almost a year. What slowed us down were equipment breakdowns, spare part delays, personnel problems, and the sheer difficulty of getting anything done that far away from a hardware store.

Drinking water was always a problem. At that time, we had not yet started our wells-to-reservoir system. We experimented with various water catchment methods. We tried tin

Top
Our sawmill.

Bottom
Floor boards made of coconut plants.

Top
View from the workers' village.

Bottom
View from Marlon's future hut.

roofs, and even plastic sheeting made into troughs that were suspended from trees. The tin roofs worked well enough, though they collected a lot of dirt and leaves. The plastic sheeting did not survive the winds. The flapping made a hell of a noise, and the water spilled out before we could collect it. When it rained, everyone would get out buckets and run to the flapping sheets, where they got more water on themselves than in the buckets. So I ordered a 27-cubic-yard galvanized steel container for the campsite. It was covered with a fine mesh screen and placed below a tin-roofed storage shed. The screen was to keep the mosquitoes and other critters out, as well as to filter the dirt and leaves from the water. The only trouble was that a certain amount of fine stuff got through, and I found myself having to clean it out by getting in the tank naked to scrub the walls that were covered with a greenish moss. After my cleaning, some people commented that they preferred the taste of the green slime water to that of water flavored by my sweaty body.

When May Day rolled around, everyone was ready for a party. Holidays in Tahiti tend to be an excuse for a feast, and Taputuarai arrived with beer, wine, mangos, bananas, papayas, watermelon, all sorts of cakes, and a huge pig. The poor thing was too much to handle, so she was thrown overboard and had to swim in over the reef herself. Work stopped for a few days while we all participated in lavish preparations, including killing the poor pig and roasting it in an earth oven. We wrapped fish in banana leaves to be cooked in the oven around the pork. We made both *mitihaari* and *mitihue* from coconuts. Young, still-green coconuts contain cool, deliciously sweet-tasting water, which doubles as a laxative if you drink too much. Older coconuts that have turned from green to brown, and have fallen on the ground before they sprouted, are split with an axe for the white meat inside. Tahitians de-husk coconuts on sharpened wooden sticks, but we used a steel spike stuck in the ground. Once the outer shell, or husk, has been removed with a sharp tool, the brown nut is exposed, it is cracked, and the thick white meat inside is ready to be grated. The traditional way to grate is to sit on a low carved wooden stool that has a protrusion with a sharp serrated steel tool attached to it. One straddles the stool, holding a half-open coconut between one's legs, and scrapes it, grates it on the serrated steel. These shavings are squeezed in a cloth to produce a creamy milk called *mitihaari*. *Mitihue* is coconut meat mixed with crushed shrimp heads and left to ferment a few days. Both are used in sauces, and the *mitihue*, potent and very fishy, really knocks your socks off.

Copra, the natural white coconut meat dried in the sun for a week or two, can be made into cooking and body oils, soaps, and perfumes. It is still farmed and sold commercially, though the industry has diminished a great deal. *Copra* used to be a major business in Polynesia, but it has declined in recent years due to the development of chemically derived detergents, soaps, and perfumes. The copra processing plant in the port of Papeete fills the air with the sweet aroma of coconut oil as a solitary reminder of the days when *copra* was king.

Zeke, Tea, and their kids came over for the May Day festivities, along with Purea, her good friend Dolly Higgins, whom we all adored, and of course Tetua the maid, who had no teeth, but an open and contagious smile. We were thrilled to see them, not to mention the numerous bottles of rum and fresh limes they brought along. The Tahitian workers, dressed in Hawaiian shirts (I didn't know they even had shirts with them), strummed their guitars and ukuleles, while I played a string attached to a stick on top of an upside-down pail. What an instrument! We ate, drank, and sang all day and half the night. Sadly, Marlon was in the States, and missed a wild party.

After a few days of rest, work resumed, but at a different pace. Teihotu loved to ride on the bulldozer, where he would sometimes doze off seated next to the driver as it rolled along. Christian continued to wreak havoc, setting free hermit crabs from Sabrina's pet crab collection, and I started to worry about the new, much slower pace that had settled in after the party. Dora announced she was ready to go home. The excitement we'd all shared at the beginning of the project seemed to be wearing off. The workers had been away from their families for months. Unfortunately, there wasn't a whole lot I could do about it. We had to get the job done, and I could only hope that a renewed spirit would develop.

Right about that time, some interesting guests arrived, providing a much-needed distraction for me, and inspiration to the others: scientists. Our Tahitian crew was at first curious, then fascinated by their scientific research on the atoll. I had tried to talk to the crew about ecology and the interconnectedness of the environment, but scientists actually conducting studies became much more inspirational than *popaa pra pra*, white man's talk. Marlon and I were absolutely devoted to preserving the environment of his island, but a bit naive about how to go about it. After all, it had been only a few years since Rachel Carson had written *The Silent Spring*; the environmental movement was in its infancy. But Marlon as developer and I as his advisor were determined to maintain the ecosystem of the atoll as well as we possibly could. We were, in a very real sense, plowing new ground.

This was years before environmental impact studies were considered, much less required. We had invited numerous scientists to come to Tetiaroa to research its various ecosystems. For them the atoll was a scientific paradise. The first to arrive was Jean-Claude Thibault, a young ornithologist from the Musée National d'Histoire Naturelle in France. Tetiaroa had, and thanks to Marlon, still has, a very significant colony of seabirds living on several of its *motus*. These birds are not only important in their own right, but they also play a prominent role in the economic life of Tahiti. They act as "guides" for the tuna fishing fleet by "showing" the fishermen where schools of tuna can be found. Jean-Claude actually counted the birds of Tetiaroa, noting their species and their health conditions. He found that there were over 30,000 seabirds living on eight of the *motus*, primarily Noddys and Boobys, but also magnificent Great Frigates, regal Herons, chubby Plovers, and small, quick Tatlers and Terns. Most of the birds feed in the open ocean and nest in low branches on the beach or in the sand itself. Jean Claude recommended that none of the eight nesting motus be visited, let alone inhabited by humans. Hundreds of eggs were underfoot or within arm's reach and would be harmed. That changed our plans quite a bit, as we had initially envisioned specific activities taking place on several of the islets. It would not be the last time my original plans for Tetiaroa had to be changed. I'm pleased to note that Thibault has been conducting periodic follow-up studies on Tetiaroa since his first survey almost 35 years ago, and the bird life is still thriving.

Back on the runway, things were still going slowly. The grading, compacting, and surfacing was taking longer than we anticipated. Although the Meherio had brought us a second dump truck and a grader, one of them and/or the bulldozer always seemed to break down. This was not a surprise. After all, they were old machines operating in salt air conditions with inadequate maintenance even before arriving on the island. We didn't have a proper machine shop, and our drivers were not the best mechanics. Sometimes Taputuarai was forced to send for a mechanic, and getting one to the atoll was never easy. It could take weeks. I'd call Tea by radio. She'd call Taputuarai's office in Papeete and wait until someone was free. Then we'd have to locate a boat and wait for good weather. And then we'd have to get the poor fellow across the reef. But that wasn't all. Once on the *motu*, the mechanic would have to diagnose the problem and hope he had brought the right tools and parts with him. If not, we'd have to start all over, radio Papeete to place the order, and have it delivered. Sometimes the mechanic would have to wait for the part as long as a week. That caused project delays and cost Taputuarai a sizeable amount of money. Fortunately, I had arranged for Taputuarai's men to work for me (that is to say, for Marlon) when they weren't working on the airstrip. With their help, we'd continue gathering and stocking building materials for our little hotel. Some of Taputuarai's men were soaking logs and leaves in the lagoon, while others wove *niau* for the roofs and walls. A team searched other *motus* for trees that could be used as rafters.

Marlon came back later that summer. In spite of minimal developments on the airstrip since his last visit, he was not discouraged; in fact, he was pleased that, in general, things were going as well as they were. He had lived in Tahiti long enough to know how rough it could be to get things done, and he sympathized with my plight. During his brief stay on that particular trip, he proposed a new site for the hotel. Originally, the hotel was to have been built at the location of our campsite. Marlon may have been reassessing the location because of its current state. It was littered with broken-down trucks and construction debris. Despite the obvious disarray, the site was comfortable, because it had been lived in. Copra workers had used it before we were there, and we had repaired their huts and were reusing them. We all felt very much at home there. The breezes were constant, the views magnificent, and we were sheltered from cold winds that occasionally blew in from the south. Marlon and I had envisioned the hotel's main building on the spot overlooking the shimmering lagoon where we had enjoyed so many meals and drinks during our planning phase. I still liked that idea, but much to my surprise, Marlon seemed to be changing his mind.

One day at sunrise during this particular visit, I came upon him on the beach outside my tent. "Bernie, you've got to see this," Marlon said. We walked to a point at the northern tip of the island, and indeed, the view of the sun rising in the east behind the *motus* was spellbinding. A silvery-pink to red-orange light shone over the lagoon, and Marlon turned to me. "This is where the hotel should be."

Despite the beautiful scene, I had my doubts, because the place seemed too open and therefore too exposed. There were not many trees. A few at the water's edge had exposed roots in the water, making it evident that the land had been washed away some time ago. The sandy soil was covered with a thin black film I could not explain. But Marlon had made up his mind. He wanted this site. It was useless to argue. It was his passion over my reason. We were not unlike young lovers.

"I know what you want, but it's too risky," I said.
"I know, but this is what I want."
"But it's dangerous."
"But it's going to be so nice."
"A lot is involved; think of the future…"
"You know I'm going to have my way, so don't fight me."

Right then and there, I knew I had to give in. Discouraged because I could not think of an argument that would change his mind, I relented. In retrospect I have to admit that I didn't know for sure that this site would indeed be any more dangerous in a heavy storm than the one we had planned originally. I thought I'd let him have his way for a day or two, then approach the subject again. That tactic usually worked. It didn't work that time. It was give in or give up and go home.

So I changed the plans, and moved not only the hotel main building, kitchen, and bar, but also the bungalows, the wells, piping, sanitation facilities, reception hut, firefighting and electrical systems all to the north of the runway, 500 yards from camp. I wrote to Ron back in the office in Los Angeles: "NEW SITE! I'm sending sketches. Start new plans." Fortunately, the building plans themselves didn't have to be changed. They just had to be repositioned on the site plan. But changes meant changing the size of the plumbing and electrical systems, as well as their positions on the site. I set about scouting and staking new building locations

May Day celebration. Zeke, Tea, and their son Kavika in the foreground.

Top
Tetua on bass, Tonio on guitar, and Kavika looking on.

Bottom
Drying laundry for May Day.

Top
Our earth oven. Breadfruit and fish.

Bottom
Our kitchen hut.

Top
Copra, the white meat inside the coconuts.

Bottom
Breadfruit ready to eat.

north of the runway. I was irritated, but tried not to show it. In a way, it was a whole new project for me and I took the challenge as I always did. It didn't take long to find solutions to some of the problems I foresaw on the new site. For instance, I placed the floor of the main building 3 feet above the natural grade and put most of the sleeping huts up on 4-foot-high *piloti*, pylons, in case wind-driven high water would come in from the lagoon.

Marlon left satisfied with the new hotel site. Dora, who had been on Tetiaroa for several months, decided it was time for her to leave as well. Her pottery studio in Los Angeles beckoned, and she wanted to prepare for a sale. As a matter of fact, the whole crew was ready to go home. I started to hear a lot of the Tahitian *fiu*. *Fiu* might be applied to a work situation, an island's claustrophobia, a relationship, or even a marriage, and translates into "I've had it. I'm leaving." No doubt, some of Taputuarai's crew members were feeling *fiu*. I, on the other hand, was not. In spite of the problems incurred by the new hotel site, and the work the alterations to the plans would mean for me, I was still entranced by Tetiaroa. I was even giddy with the responsibility of getting the project done. In fact, I was in heaven. I was designing and building my own world. What an experience! I could not have been happier, despite occasional reversals and delays. I was completely enamored with the physicality of Tetiaroa, and enthralled with its natural setting. I must admit, wearing a bathing suit or a *pareu* all day long out in the sun beats wearing a suit and tie at the office every day. One of my surprising joys was riding in an outrigger canoe across the lagoon, looking at the backs of the Tahitians as they paddled those canoes with easy strokes. It was wonderful to watch their muscles rippling under their wet skin, their rhythm somehow intoxicating. Either I was mesmerized by the splendor of sweating dark skin, or the sun was getting to me.

Whenever I could, I'd go snorkeling with my underwater camera to shoot bright orange, purple-and-electric blue, or black-and-white striped fish gliding in and out of rose-colored coral heads. There were blue lipped clams, *pahuas,* that smiled up at me, and then clamped shut as I tried to dislodge them with a screwdriver. I loved to wander the island and gather stuff that had drifted in the night before. I had decorated the interior of the office hut with half coconut shells hanging from the rafters. I had removed their husks, revealing three small holes on the shell at the spot where the coconut had been attached to the tree. To me, the holes resembled two beady eyes and an O-shaped mouth, and each shell developed a personality all its own. I had given them names, greeted them, and talked to them. Call me crazy! Maybe the sun *was* getting to me.

I thought those coconuts would make wonderful ornaments at the hotel. We could make use of other found material as well. We discovered that the spines of palm fronds did not rot. When the leaf was stripped, the spines could be woven into complex patterns, and used as screens. One-to two-foot-wide conch shells would make marvelous bathroom sinks. Glass buoys, small colored light bulbs, barnacle covered bottles that floated into shore from the ocean, and driftwood were plentiful and would be festive. We didn't have to buy furniture like tables and chairs from catalogues because we would be hiring local craftsmen to make them right on the atoll. Even glasses and plates didn't have to be store-bought. We would use flat shells for hors d'oeuvres, and Reiko was already busily making various sizes of drinking glasses from empty beer bottles by cutting them in half with a red hot wire. She fashioned the top half of the bottles into candleholders, the bottoms into glasses. Believe me, there was an endless supply of beer bottles for her to work with.

Speaking of beer, as much as I loved those Tahitians, they were scary when they got drunk. I let them drink beer on weekends, but I was the only one who had the key to the beer locker. I remember one group came to my tent in the middle of the night and demanded the key. They were already drunk and had run out of beer. I was frightened, as they could have easily overpowered me. They had machetes and were angry. I got up and out of the tent and feigned real anger to cover my fear, and shouted at the top of my lungs: *"Va t'en!* Get out of here! *Va t'en!"* Luckily, I eventually succeeded in staring them down. First one, then another sheepishly left, grumbling all the way down to the beach. Getting back into my tent, I realized that I was trembling! It had been the first time, and gratefully the last, that I had to yell at my workers.

Christmas was fast approaching and I had to make arrangements for the workers to go home. I had promised Dora that I, too, would be back in Los Angeles for the holidays, which meant that the *motu* would be left empty for at least a week. I knew that would be risky because of potential theft. By that time we had a lot of valuable equipment on the island and I didn't want to take a chance on some of it being "borrowed." I was not into taking risks. We would need a caretaker. While discussing the dilemma with Tea, she suggested her mother might be interested in going out to the island. Purea loved the atoll and could bring her long time friends Dolly and Tetua along. They were the perfect crew to "babysit" the island and they quickly agreed. Purea loved to fish, Dolly to cook, and Tetua would look after things in general and watch over Purea's two dachshunds. Dolly was a loving, warm-hearted, good-natured, and funny woman of ample girth. She lived in Moorea and everybody knew and loved her. Whenever there was an anniversary, a wedding, a birthday, or even a funeral, Dolly's friends wanted her around. She knew everyone by name, knew where to get everything necessary to stock a large gathering, was a terrific help in a pinch and a fantastic cook, too. It was agreed, Purea, Dolly, Tetua, and the dachshunds would be the caretakers of Tetiaroa while I was gone.

On the flight from Papeete to Los Angeles, my seat partner next to the window was a young Tahitian girl, perhaps fifteen years old, on her way to Paris to visit relatives for the

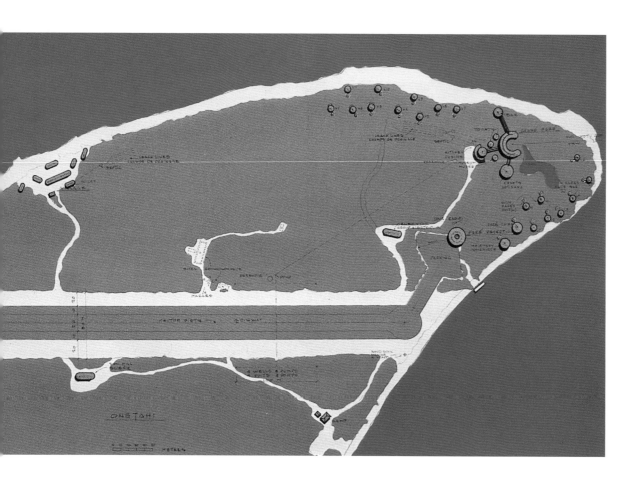

The new hotel site.

holidays. This was her first time out of Tahiti and she was very excited, to go to a big city like Paris. As we approached LAX at sunset, she looked out the window and saw city lights for the first time in her life. "Look," she exclaimed, "they have illuminated millions of Christmas trees!"

Home for Christmas! I had missed two holiday seasons while in Tahiti in 1970 and '71, and was really happy to be back in Los Angeles with my family again. I still find that certain frantic hustle and bustle that takes place around that time of year contagious. Even in Southern California, where there is not a hint of snow, I feel captured by a holiday spirit like the one I knew growing up in New York. For me, Los Angeles becomes invigorating at Christmas time. One actually sees pedestrians in a city that seems made for cars, not humans. The pace on the sidewalk is brisk and purposeful, not laid back as usual. For a short time, I almost forgot about my lagoon and my little island. All the decorated store windows, the shopping and colorful packages, Christmas trees tied to car roofs, and bright lights in front yards temporarily transported me back home from my South Pacific world.

I was happy to get dressed up and go to parties to see old acquaintances. One evening, Dora and I invited some friends for cocktails. I knew that Marlon didn't like to meet new people, but I asked him anyway, and drop in he did, in a most unusual way. A sliding door to the living room had been left partially open so guests could come and go with ease, and the room was full. People were standing around or sitting in chairs or on cushions on the floor. It was dark except for the Christmas tree in a corner. At one point, I suddenly spotted Marlon seated cross-legged between two of my friends, chatting away. He had snuck in through the sliding door on all fours, and had simply sat down and started talking to the first people he came across. Dressed in a black turtleneck sweater and dark velour jacket, he blended right in. No one had even noticed him. After a while, he realized he wasn't going to be the center of attention, so he got comfortable and started mixing and mingling and telling amusing stories. He recognized my physiologist friend Alan, got into a conversation with him, and ended up inviting him to Tetiaroa. I was discovering that Marlon, who barely got through high school, loved to be surrounded by scientists, writers, and intellectuals whenever he could. He enjoyed engaging in conversations with people he could learn from. He was good at asking penetrating questions. He was at ease and gracious. I could tell he was having a good time that night. As the evening came to a close, he kissed us on both cheeks, thanked Dora and me, and then, before I knew it, disappeared. He probably crawled out on his hands and knees, the very same way he came in. Here was a man who rarely left his bedroom, avoided restaurants, and traveled in disguise. His very presence was so magnetic that people would stop in their tracks when they saw him, and conversations would cease when he stepped into a room. It wasn't that he was a Hollywood celebrity; he simply had a magnetic force that was hard to hide. That night at Christmas though, Marlon, a man who couldn't avoid being in the limelight no matter how hard he tried, had made himself invisible.

Purea's "babysitting" job lasted a bit longer than the week I had originally anticipated. I had returned to Papeete from L.A., but high seas were making it impossible to disembark over the reef at Tetiaora. I was having a heck of a time getting the crew to go back to work after the holidays as well. It seemed like any excuse the men could come up with was enough to prevent them from returning. Their families missed them, the job was taking too long, someone was sick...

Over on the island, Purea, Dolly, and Tatua were running out of essentials, cigarettes and rum, in particular. Tea went to the Bata shoe store in Papeete and pleaded with the owner, Gilbert Letty, to fly over in his small two-seat plane and drop supplies for them. Gilbert was only too happy to have some fun. Every few days Tea would make up a package consisting of tobacco, rum, limes, fresh baguettes, and a newspaper. The plane would fly low out of the clouds and buzz the airstrip to alert the women of his arrival. He would then make a rolling turn over the campsite, cut the throttle almost to the point of stalling, lower the flaps, and push the package out the window aiming for the thatch-roof of the office hut in hopes that it would break the fall. He missed his mark often, but remarkably, nothing ever broke. The three women would wave their *pareus* madly, laughing and dancing on the beach as Gilbert flew off, tipping his wings in farewell. As long as they had their goodies, the babysitters were happy to stay.

After about two frustrating weeks in Papeete, I was finally able to round up the crew and a boat to get us back on the island in good weather. As we came across the lagoon, we were greeted by three grinning survivors, each wearing a leafy *courone* on her pretty head. They had made leis for all of us, and spread out a marvelous meal of delicate smelts, lobster, and fresh coconut bread just out of the earth oven. It was a fantastic homecoming, and the men were happy to be back after all.

The runway had to be finished. Coconut trees had been felled and the trunks separated from the leaves. Both had been allowed to dry and then put in the lagoon to soak up salt water as a preservative. They were, after all, our main construction material. Root balls had been dug out, as they would rot and cause depressions in the runway. It was a pleasure to see right across the island, from lagoon to lagoon. The top layer of topsoil had been sifted for bits of coral, shells, and other debris, and then replaced on the runway. Now, grading and compacting had to be accomplished.

Top
My friends, the coconuts.

Bottom
A coconut grater seems to be climbing a tree.

The final touch on the airstrip was spreading topsoil and planting grass. I had ordered grass seed from Hawaii after conferring with the authorities in Papeete and with the U.S. Agriculture Department. The challenge had been to find a type of grass that would grow in calcareous sand, wouldn't spread wildly and could be confined to the runway, would withstand airplane traffic and not require much upkeep. We didn't want the grass to take over the island, and we had precious little water to feed it. It was a tall order, and when the suggested blend arrived, we had high hopes. After planting, I went out to the runway every morning to inspect the little green shoots as they sprouted through the sandy topsoil. Pretty soon a lovely green cast appeared, and I was delighted.

Top
Making sure the airstrip is straight.

Bottom
Separating the leaves from the trunks.

Top
Driving the leaves for composting.

Bottom
Sifting the topsoil for bits of coral and roots.

Top
Grading and compacting the runway.

Bottom
The runway stretches from lagoon to lagoon.

In late January, engineers from Civil Aviation came over by boat to inspect our airfield. They walked it, tested its compaction, and measured its width and length. The wind-socks had not arrived, so I volunteered my red *pareu*, and it did the job. Taputuarai had done fantastic work; the inspection went swimmingly, and we celebrated with plenty of champagne.

We were now ready for an official test flight. One gorgeous, clear morning, Gilbert Letty, our supply pilot, was waiting to take off from Papeete in his little plane when we radioed him that we were ready for him. Sabrina sat in as co-pilot, and on her lap she carried her little dog, Poopie. A half-hour after we had called them, we spotted a speck on the horizon. As the plane approached, it made one pass over the runway to check it out (Poopie peed in Sabrina's lap), and turned to land. I held my breath. A perfect three point landing! Everyone ran to the plane cheering and shouting!

On the one hand, Marlon couldn't wait to fly in, but his fear of flying in a small plane held him back from actually boarding. He was used to flying on big transcontinental airplanes, but on long flights, he usually had Alice accompany him and hold his hand. Although Gilbert's little craft had had no problem landing or taking off again, what about an Air Tahiti's nine-passenger Britten-Norman, or a twenty-passenger Twin Otter? Marlon was not going to be the first to take a chance on those larger planes, especially as they had never landed on our new runway. So the very first commercial flight to Tetiaroa carried fruits and vegetables, a half a dozen workers, Dora, but no Marlon. For those of us on the ground, it was a wonderful sight to see that plane circle the island and come in for a flawless landing. The Civil Aviation guys still on the island were delighted as well, and got a ride home on the next flight back to Papeete.

Once Marlon had been reassured that airplanes could land safely on our runway, he forced himself to overcome his anxiety and hopped aboard the next flight, with good old Alice, Tarita, and the kids in tow. He had insisted that the owner of Air Tahiti himself pilot the plane. The owner was more than happy to do so, especially as he was eager to check out the runway himself. Marlon was all smiles as he strode off the plane dressed in his floppy old shorts, tee shirt, and straw hat. He, all of us really–seven Tahitians, myself, and some old broken-down equipment–had accomplished something uncommonly demanding in building that runway, something that had been the butt of much derision among the naysayers back in Papeete.

Champagne for us all!

Top
Sabrina arrives with Gilbert Letti.
The first plane on Tetiaroa.

Bottom
Marlon arrives on next plane to
land on Tetiaroa.

Dora greets Marlon and the pilot, who was also the owner of Air Tahiti.

Top
Dora, Teihotu, the pilot, and Joel's
girlfriend, Moya.

Bottom
Marlon shaking hands with an official from the Civil Aviation.
Teihotu in the foreground.

Airstrip completed!

Early 1973

I NEED HELP

A Bloody Mess
South Seas "Sirens"

While we were completing the airstrip, the workers had been simultaneously stockpiling coconut logs and leaves we'd use as roofing materials. The Alaskan sawmill had been set up, and stacks of lumber set out to dry. New construction crews were now arriving by plane, so that construction on the main buildings could begin. Some brought their wives along, which made for a pleasant community of us Tetiaroans working together. We had enlarged the workers' quarters to allow for all the new people. The whole dynamic on the island changed. My original camp evolved for the third time. It was still a campsite, but there were more tents for visitors, and a lot more people to feed. Marlon was present more often now, sometimes accompanied by his family and friends or by more scientists he had invited. Unintentionally, Reiko and Dora became hostesses. Marlon's children Christian and Miko came back from L.A., this time with a tutor. Our campsite would be full one day and empty the next as visitors came and went, but I kept about my business, and enjoyed the suspense of never really knowing who or what to expect at mealtimes! When a plane departed after delivering construction supplies, its passengers were given lists of things we needed from town. On one occasion, Dora went to Papeete for the day. Marlon had given her a shopping list for food for the evening meal and the list included a bottle of rum. When Dora's plane got back that evening, Marlon discovered that Dora had forgotten his rum and yelled at her. She got so fed up, she took a swing at him and knocked his hat off. I'd never seen Marlon with quite such an expression—surprise, anger, confusion, and amusement all at once. Dora was not to be reckoned with, and Marlon, who could have decked her, controlled himself.

During the early stages of construction it became clear that I would need some help. Marlon agreed. I was burdened with too many things to do at once, and it was compromising my work on the design of the hotel. My responsibilities were all exciting, but there were just too many of them. I had to interface with my office in Los Angeles, where people were busy redesigning the plumbing, sewage and electrical systems to handle the recent change in site location. I was the one ordering spare parts for the sawmill and pumps when they broke down, and I was ordering construction materials such as cement, reinforcing rods and galvanized nails that had to be brought in from Papeete. As stated in our contract, Taputuarai supplied labor, but not materials. I was the one supervising construction and making design changes as problems came to light on a daily basis. I was also assisting the scientists in their studies on atoll ecology. And I was even the one taking care of the payroll. Marlon had me paying all the bills, including Tarita's grocery bills at the Chinese store in Punaauia. At the beginning of the project Marlon had taken me to the Bank of Tahiti and arranged for me to sign his name on all his accounts. I ended up overseeing all of Marlon's accounts in Polynesia. On top of that I was using his friends, and mine, as free labor. Tea, her mother, Dolly, Zeke, Michele, as well as Dora, were all contributing to the project, but were not on any payroll. In a way it was more like a family business than a straight commercial enterprise, and I was the head of the whole family!

Any and all of this I had to coordinate from an 8 x 8-foot tent I shared with my wife and daughter. The office hut had been fixed up as a guest cottage, and a home for the radio transmitter and whatever paraphernalia the researchers and kids would leave around, and so I had no choice but to move operations into our tent. I sat on a box at a makeshift desk made from a large crate. My files and drawings were kept in a plastic garbage can that I had brought from L.A. I had learned my lesson on that first survey trip: everything gets wet going over the reef and crossing the lagoon, and inside a tent every time it rains! On the other side of our inflatable mattress were two well-used camp chairs and the suitcases which served as our chest of drawers and library. A kerosene lamp provided light at night. Talk about burning the midnight oil! I was staying up till 2:00 or 3:00 in the morning with my interminable lists of things to do and problems to solve.

The concept of introducing non-indigenous plants, animals, and house pets to the atoll was of major concern to me. Should we allow decorative flowers such as bougainvillea to be grown? Which plants would spread out of control and take over indigenous plants? We had entertained the idea of raising chickens and pigs to provide meat and eggs for the village. How would they affect the environment? What about the economics of raising animals, versus buying and flying in meat, chicken, and eggs from Tahiti. What about pets? Sabrina had brought Poopie to the island, why couldn't everyone else? Our vow to protect the environment raised so many practical and theoretical questions that had to be answered. I had to set up a monitoring and policing system once Marlon and I decided what the rules should be. The planes would have to be sprayed with insecticide before leaving Papeete for the atoll. As a practical matter, who would do the spraying and who would make sure it was done? We had access to environmental specialists, but they didn't know anything more than I did about the practical and financial aspects of designing a sustainable yet benign system for living on an uninhabited atoll in the middle of the ocean. We were all learning as we went along, and to put it mildly, it was a bit of a bumpy road.

My role as the neophyte, sun-burnt *popaa* with a funny hat had somehow, slowly, changed to my becoming "papa Bernard," the fellow who was there all the time and could be counted on to take care of any problem that came up, big or small, night or day. One day, as I was checking over a list of what to do the next day (lists, interminable lists), I heard a scream coming from the jungle, ran out of my tent and found a young girl, blood streaming from her hair, being pursued by a man wielding a machete! She ran up to me, screaming that her father was going to kill her. Indeed he almost had. The girl had an open gash in her scalp. Someone held the father back as I wrapped a rag around the girl's head trying to stop the flow of blood. I was in shock, too. What the hell was going on and what was I going to do about it? Her head was a mess of matted hair and blood. A crowd had gathered, and there was yelling, crying and pushing, which only added to the girl's hysteria. I changed the towel, this time grabbing a clean one, wrapped it around her head and chin as tightly as I could without choking her to death, and got on the radio for an emergency *evacuation sanitaire*. Within thirty minutes the plane arrived, although it seemed like hours that I held that girl in my arms hoping and praying she wouldn't pass out. Off she went with her father on board. It turned out that the crazed father had caught the girl in the bushes with a young man and had completely lost it. I was forced into a position of being medic, cop, prosecutor, and judge. I fired the father, of course, and when I found out who the man in the bushes was, I fired him as well. Fortunately the young girl survived, but I never saw any of them again.

The hotel was to open in 10-12 months. It was time to think about professionals to run the place for Marlon, as well as who would be hiring the staff. Marlon left it all up to me, because he distrusted anyone he didn't know, in particular people he had to pay to recommend people he didn't know. The whole issue of trust and control was coming to a head. Marlon had tested me many times, so he trusted me. I had access to his home and his bank accounts, but my role as planner, architect, and construction supervisor had turned into something much more. He had forsaken some control. I was the mother giving birth to his dream on the atoll! "Yes," Marlon said when I told him that, "but never forget I am the father."

After discussing my workload with Marlon, and admitting that I was a bit loaded with my manifold responsibilities, I hired Omer's daughter Michele to be my assistant. While we were building the runway, she had volunteered to help with chores that Tea was unable to do in town, or chores I felt could not dump on Tea because I had relied on her good will for too long. Michele and I had developed an easy-going relationship. I found her to be honest, intelligent, and resourceful, and I found that I could depend on her even at the last minute. At the time, Michele was living in Papeete with her former schoolmate and best friend, Tiare Higgins, by now a UTA airline stewardess. Michele knew her way around the town because of her father's yacht, and was familiar with all the hardware stores and warehouses. This was important, as one could waste half a day searching for simple items such as batteries for a flashlight. Michele's responsibilities were to buy construction materials and supplies for our campsite, as well as to take care of visitors, both in Papeete and on Onetahi. When archaeologist Dr. Sinoto from Hawaii, or Dr. Fosberg and Dr. Sachet from the Smithsonian Institution arrived, Michele arranged for their hotels, met them at the airport, got them to our campsite, and generally watched over them during their visit. Some of these turned out magnificently, such as the Fosberg/Sachet visit, which produced a report on the ecological reconnaissance of Tetiaroa. When it was published in July of 1973, it became our Bible.

After I hired Michele, I was spending a day or two each week in Papeete, and my bedroom at Marlon's became my in-town office. When Michele first came to Marlon's house and I told her that my bedroom would be our office, she walked in, sat on the bed, and looked around with an enigmatic smile. I remembered then that her father had sold the house to Marlon, and that my bedroom had been hers when she was a little girl.

I started to interview potential hotel managers and some permanent staff, particularly a mechanic we needed to be a jack-of-all-trades for the hotel operation. Back when we were building the airstrip, volunteers like Michele and Tiare were glad to work with me just for the experience of helping to preserve a beautiful atoll. As an airline stewardess, Tiare would purchase items in Los Angeles and get them to us within three days rather than three weeks. It was a pleasure for me to have eager young hands to help around camp. One of them, a young American named Joel, had sailed to Tahiti with a group of friends and was immediately captivated. The Tahitian government, however, did not look with pleasure on "yachties" who sailed in and didn't move on, particularly those who had no visible means of income. Tourists were only permitted to stay in Tahiti for twenty-one days without a visa. Sailboats and crew could ride out the hurricane season from April to July, but they had to leave soon after. Visiting sailors had been getting around these rules for ages by starting a family with a local woman. Joel didn't have a family, and so I gave him a temporary work contract. I'm glad I did, as he could read architectural plans, had some construction background, and had unusually acute language skills. He picked up Tahitian immediately, and I'll never forget his lovely Tahitian girlfriend Moya, whom he brought to Tetiaroa. I can still picture her dressed in her skimpy *pareu*, her long hair swaying gently in the evening breezes as she sang poignant songs while accompanying herself on a guitar. It was not too long before she got pregnant. The baby would have been our first native Tetiaroan, but sadly, on doctor's orders, the couple had to leave to be closer to a hospital. I was sorry to see them go. Now I really needed permanent help on the island.

On several occasions we had hired a German mechanic who worked at the Moorea Club Med. He went by the name of Klaus, and before he got stuck at the Club Med, he had been in the French Foreign Legion. Captain Siki would bring him out to the reef, and we fetched him in our Zodiac. Good old Siki continued to come to our aid when no one else was available, sometimes at the very last moment. He was one of the few people I could rely on. I was not so sure about relying on Klaus, because I knew that French Legionnaires were accepted into service without any background checks. The men took on a new name, and with it a new identity. No questions asked. As far as the rest of the world is concerned, they have no past. That worried me. I knew nothing about Klaus, not even whether that was his real name. He could have been an axe murderer. He was a big, barrel-chested, beer-bellied fellow with a booming basso voice and a thin curly beard. He spoke English and French, and seemed to fit the jack-of-all-trades job description. He came with good recommendations from the Club Med, but I was not sure. Marlon, who found him an interesting personality study, said "OK, offer him a job."

After three years on Tetiaroa, Marlon and I understood that our original dream to create a self-supporting village would not be possible. We agreed that the small hotel would have to supply all of the island's revenue. We would have to depend on the hotel as our one commercial venture; therefore, the people involved in running the hotel became terribly important. Marlon and I concurred that sensitivity, strength of character, patience and honesty, coupled with a keen business sense, were key attributes for the hotel managers we were looking for.

Zeke and Tea introduced me to their friend Ivan, the general manager of the Maeva Beach Hotel, the UTA airlines hotel in Papeete. Ivan said he was looking for a new challenge, and I saw right away that he was bright and charming. He spoke six languages and had a solid background in hotel management and marketing. Originally from Switzerland, he had lived in Tahiti for several years and was familiar with the rules and regulations of the hotel business. He knew several travel agents, many of whom were the wholesalers who booked blocks of rooms and airplane seats. He seemed perfect for the job. Marlon, however, wanted his personal travel agent, Rosette, to do the hotel marketing. She had done marketing in French Polynesia for years and was on familiar terms with everyone at the airlines, the managers, the pilots, and the ground crews. But most importantly, Marlon had known her for a long time and trusted her. And indeed, Rosette could make miracles happen. Once she got me on a plane from LAX to Papeete at the last minute without a ticket! I knew her and was fond of her, but I felt strongly that one person needed to be overseeing everything: the operations of the village, the management and marketing of the hotel, hiring and firing, and organizing tours. I thought Ivan was the perfect candidate. If anything, he was over-qualified. But, as so often before, Marlon didn't want anything to do with strangers, no matter how qualified. If Rosette would do the marketing, we'd need a Tahitian to manage the hotel. We couldn't find anyone with skills that could rival those of Ivan. Marlon got so frustrated through the course of our discussions about this that he actually demanded, "Bernie, you do it!" I had absolutely no desire to run a hotel, nor did I have a clue as to how to do it, and so I refused. We ended up having a big fight over it. "Look," I said, "someone has to be the big cheese around here every single day. It isn't going to be you, or Tarita, or me, because none of us could possibly handle it. We'd screw it up royally." Finally he relented "OK, let's give this Ivan a trial run. I don't want to talk about it anymore."

Ivan was eager to get going. His wife, Evie, was an interior designer with an interest in Tahitian crafts. It seemed like a perfect fit. I liked them, and they had fresh ideas about how a hotel on Tetiaroa could distinguish itself from other small hotels in Polynesia. Ivan admired Dora's sketches of the flora and fauna, and her abstract sand sculptures that would be used as concrete molds for our outdoor bar. He found her work fresh and creative, and felt that it captured an oceanic feeling perfect for the hotel. He asked her to create some graphic designs for the hotel logo and brochure. I was relieved that Ivan could take over some of my work as well, and was delighted to hand him the chore of ordering bathroom fixtures, kitchen and bar equipment, everything from refrigerators to an eight-burner stove.

While the construction on Tetiaroa was being completed, Ivan and Evie lived near Marlon's house in Punaauia. Ivan didn't have to be on the atoll for his work, so Marlon's house became a convenient place for meetings for all of us. First it was Michele and I in the bedroom, then Ivan,

Michele, and I in the living room, and finally Ivan, Evie, Dora, Michele, and I, and occasionally Marlon, in the dining room for meetings. Tarita was not pleased. The house had become our headquarters. Always trying to make Tarita happy, Marlon promised to build her a separate house in the front yard and it was not very long before he did. She lives there to this day.

One morning, I walked into Marlon's bedroom and found him sitting in bed with a dopey smile, as if he had been caught with his hand in the cookie jar. Hundreds of $100 bill wrappers were on the floor and on his bed around him.

"What did you do now, Bud, rob a bank?"
"Something like that. Here, take one," he offered.
"Thanks a lot, but that's only a wrapper," I quipped.
"I know, and that's all you're going to get if I find out you tell anyone about this."

He had hidden a huge amount of money in Alice's travel bag without her knowledge. It was illegal to import more than a few thousand dollars, and she was mad as hell when she found out that Marlon had tricked her into smuggling money through customs. But we were way over budget on Tetiaroa, and Marlon had gotten a hold of some money, somehow, and stuck it in her carry-on. He and Tarita had evidently been having a great old time throwing $100 bills around his room before I walked in on them that morning.

Meanwhile, over on Tetiaroa, work on the hotel progressed, and by now nearly 100 people were on the island more or less permanently. The Tahitians and their families still had their own camp on the leeward side at the other end of the island. I wasn't ever certain why they had chosen that particular site. It was so much hotter there. I wondered if it was the breeze on the windward side, facing the lagoon, that made them often wear sweaters in the evenings. Or was it because their leeward camp faced the ocean, and not the lagoon? My feeling was that they probably enjoyed the sound of the crashing waves on the reef, which reminded them of home. Perhaps they had chosen that side to be as far away from us *popaas* as possible. It was interesting to watch their camp develop, and quite different from the way I, an American architect, would have imagined it. Everything was bunched together with all the buildings within earshot of one another. A large, open central hut served as a dining hall as well as a general meeting place. The kitchen building and separate sleeping huts for men and women were close together. There were no individual beds in the sleeping huts, just platforms upon which a group would sleep. When I asked the Tahitians about this, they replied that they don't like to sleep alone, and are afraid of the dark and of *tupapa'us*. They had built three bungalows for married couples. They were not private, but rather, tightly woven into the small village instead. The Tahitians didn't put emphasis on privacy as a *popaa* would.

Sketch of reception interior.

INTERIOR - RECEPTION

Top
Klaus repairing equipment.

Bottom
Dora's sand-sculptured concrete panels for the bar.

Starting construction on a bungalow.

I was reminded how culture, custom, and habit strongly affect one's sense of space, safety, and comfort. As an architect, this is a good lesson to remember. Marlon, who never liked that the Tahitians were so far away from the rest of us, would sometimes wander off in the evenings when he heard drums playing in their village. He was a fantastic bongo player, and would join in their music. Once he got started, he'd lose himself in a trance-like state, much to the delight and utter amusement of the Tahitians. Once he'd mastered their beats, there was no stopping him. They would go faster and faster, and he would not only keep up, but had fun beating them at their own beats.

One of the most interesting people who ever came to Tetiaroa was an American ichthyologist named Dr. Jack Randle from the University of Hawaii. A specialist in marine life, he had discovered and named several new species of fish. He had done research all over the Pacific and had become an expert on a specific disease called ciguatera. Cigua-toxins affect mammals, including humans, who eat fish infected by ciguatera. The fish acquire the toxin by eating a particular green algae. They then serve as the carriers of the disease, but they themselves do not become infected. Humans, however, can become extremely ill from the toxin, and have been known to die from eating contaminated fish. Ciguatera affects the nervous system so that the affected person's skin becomes incredibly itchy; the joints ache horribly, and for a long time. As a young man, Tea's brother Johnny got so sick eating a fish poisoned with ciguatera that he never ate fish again. To this day, Johnny lives with his family on a remote island surrounded by fish which he does not eat.

On Tetiaroa, we were particularly interested in learning if there was ciguatera in the lagoon. We were contemplating starting a turtle hatchery, and we were going to feed the turtles fish from the lagoon or the waters just outside the reef, so it was important to find out if the lagoon was contaminated. Jack was to find out if turtles reacted to the toxin like mammals or like fish. When Jack asked for volunteers, he had no trouble getting them. He did an experiment in the lagoon by cordoning off a section, several meters square, which contained a typical sampling of fish population feeding next to the reef. He used a weighted fine net to trap them, and then stunned them with a mild drug made from nuts from the *hotu* tree that he had learned were used by ancient Polynesians in fishing. They would put ground *hotu* nuts in the lagoon and wait for the drugged fish to float up to the surface to be gathered up. As we were collecting our stunned fish in buckets, an unusually big wave washed over the reef spreading the drug solution over a larger area. We were immediately surrounded by drifting fish of every size and color, and as the solution was becoming more and more diluted by the wave, the fish began to wake up and proceeded to jump wildly out of our hands. They also jumped out of the plastic buckets and almost all of them swam merrily away. It was a ridiculous situation. There we were standing shoulder deep in the lagoon, surrounded by jumping fish. We busted up laughing, including Jack. It's a good thing that the fish count was not all that important, and that Jack had a good sense of humor. When the buckets were brought to shore with the reduced collection, he photographed, sized, and noted the species of those that remained, later removing and bagging their liver and viscera to be taken to a lab in town.

Jack also collected fish outside the reef and speared several large red snapper for sampling. He always worked with a partner clutching a lethal-looking spear gun, on the look-out for sharks or barracuda. Jack had had some close calls getting distracted while concentrating on collecting fish, but had learned his lessons. Lesson one: always dive with a partner; lesson two: wear a black-and-white-striped wetsuit and try to look like a large fish. What Jack actually resembled was an escaped convict who had been washed in among the coral. That black-and-white-striped suit was just about the funniest thing I've ever seen, especially magnified underwater. Jack and his partner were terrific divers, which made it safe for me to dive with them, as I was not a certified diver. Our equipment was simple: a compressed air bottle and regulator, a mask, snorkel, and fins. We had no buoyancy vests or wetsuits to struggle with, as the water was always warm. Except for Jack, who wore his convict outfit.

The reef was abundant with colorful life. We learned from Jack that the parrot fish, the most colorful of fish, turns itself from female to male and fertilizes its own eggs! While on Tetiaroa, Jack made some marvelous discoveries. Some of them were not so welcome. "See all those sea cucumbers in the lagoon near the camp site? They are drawn by nutrient-rich effluent seeping into the lagoon." Our old septic tanks were leaking! "See those foamy bubbles riding on the lapping waves? It's detergent and will kill the coral." We were not living as lightly as we thought. As for ciguatera, luckily we found there was none in the lagoon or outside the reef.

There were so many things about Tetiaroa that Marlon and I wanted to investigate. He had read as much as he could about its history. Early archaeologists Verin and Emory, identified the many places of worship on Motu Rimatuu, near where Doctor William's family had lived. Marlon wanted to learn more about Onetahi. We knew Tetiaroa was reputed to have been the "playground" for the royal families of Tahiti, and had found several 3-foot-high upright coral slabs in the middle of Onetahi. What were they doing there? We had found large, non-indigenous trees indicating possible archaeological sites on our first survey trip. Zeke had introduced me to Dr. Yosihiko Sinoto from the Bishop Museum in Honolulu. He had been conducting a dig on the island of Huahine, near Bora Bora, at a new hotel site for the Bali Hai boys. When I mentioned this to Marlon, he invited Dr. Sinoto to conduct an archaeological survey of Onetahi. I suggested that he employ the help of some of his graduate students from the University of Hawaii. I also recommended adding some local Tahitian teacher trainees to the group. The students would have to pay their own way, but the experience would be invaluable to them. I suggested that they build their own shelters using materials at hand, and that they live, as much as possible, the way ancient Tahitians had, in order to get a good feel for what life had been like there before contact with Europeans.

In 1973 Dr. Sinoto arrived with five Hawaiian and six Tahitian students for three weeks of hard but interesting work ahead of them. The students were divided into two teams. One conducted walk-through searches for surface indicators such as coral slabs that had been used as back rests, coral laid in a pattern on the ground indicating ceremonial grounds, or a grouping of non-indigenous trees that may have marked a living site. The other team was given instruction in mapping the sites. Evenings were dedicated to lectures on how to conduct the fieldwork the following day. The mapping team made detailed site maps. Other students cleared the sites of branches, brush, and leaves. They probed with metal poles for coral slabs underground, and made test digs for anything they could find that would suggest former habitation. Fourteen Onetahi sites were discovered: ten of them were religious *maraes*; one was a habitation site near our camp, which was found by discovering garbage disposal mounds, or "middens"; another contained an earth oven; one consisted of a single upright stone that still remains a mystery; and the last contained the bones of a person buried in a seated position, which, as we learned, was extremely rare throughout all of Polynesia. Sabrina, fascinated with Sinoto's work and eager to work with the young students, was the one who found it.

Maraes were places of worship that usually included an altar, one or several raised platforms, and a seating area identified by the coral back rests. Their distinctive style, as well as the stone implements and pearl shell fish hooks found nearby, suggested that the people that built *maraes* on Tetiaroa came from more than one island group. The *maraes* found on Onetahi had an east/west orientation and a construction style typical to that of the Leeward Islands in the Society Islands chain. Others were typical of those of the Tuamotu Archipelago. Both island groups were hundreds of miles from Tetiaroa.

Several stone adz, heavy chisel-like tools made to fit on a wooden handle, found by Sinoto's students, were made of volcanic rock not indigenous to Tetiaroa. Their shapes represented differing origins. As each island in Polynesia had its own style of tools, this reinforced the suggestion that people from several islands had been on Onetahi. The ancient Polynesians did not make ceramics. Pottery shards, often used in dating archaelogical sites,

Jack Randle in his prison suit.

have not been discovered on the Tahitian islands. Dr. Sinoto, an expert who used fish hooks to date sites, developed methods of dating ancient Polynesian digs by examining shell-made hooks, and the evolution of their design. Through stratigraphy (the careful exposing of the chronological layers of an archaeological site) and carbon dating (the determination of age of an archaeological sample based on the rate of decay of its carbon 14), Sinoto was able to establish that pre-contact colonies of Polynesians had resided on Tetiaroa from 1500 to 1600 AD. He theorized that Tetiaroa had been a meeting place for people from several Polynesian islands, and, due to the many *maraes* that had been discovered there, he reasoned that Onetahi had been the *motu* of greatest importance. Marlon was surprised and delighted that the Onetahi digs had been such a success in their unique discoveries. He wanted to continue the explorations and make sure the sites were preserved; he asked Dr. Sinoto to come back with his students the next year and asked me to start a little museum with the artifacts we had collected.

I was particularly thrilled because my idea of including student teachers had proven beneficial for everyone. Some of the students later went on to be leaders in the cultural preservation movement in Tahiti. Dany Carlson became interested in cultural anthropology and went on to work in the Musée de Tahiti et des Isles. Toni Han graduated from the University of Hawaii in archaeology, and later worked with Dr. Sinoto at the Bishop museum in Honolulu. An added bonus for me was that Sabrina had a wonderful opportunity to learn something about archaeology at a very young age. She loved helping the students with their fieldwork, attended all the evening lectures, and even discovered the burial site. Sabrina had noticed what looked to be a bone in the sand. She carefully uncovered it with a brush, having learned the proper technique, and ran to me full of excitement, shouting, "Come look what I found — a skull!" I was proud of my little girl. Her involvement, curiosity, and joy of exploration were rewarded with an unusual discovery.

Life resumed a normal pace after the students left. We got up at six, drank coffee, ate baguettes under ever-swaying coconut trees overlooking the sparkling lagoon, and watched terns swooping down for their morning catch. Marlon slept late. We would hear the sounds of hammers and saws and motors starting up, and at times, Gilbert Letty arriving with the morning newspaper. Letty, who lived in Moorea, flew his plane to work in Papeete every day. Sometimes, just for the fun of it, he would take a pre-work detour and drop in for coffee. I noticed that Reiko paid him very special attention on these visits. He would bring her fresh croissants, and they would sit by themselves on the beach having their breakfast. Soon his trips became more frequent, and after a short time they became a daily affair. Not infrequently, Letty and Reiko would disappear directly into her tent, not taking time for coffee, and come out grinning. It was a sight to see. No one said anything, but as his plane took off after his morning visit, Reiko would run after it like a puppy after its master. He'd tip his wing to say *adieu* as he flew over the shimmering lagoon on to Papeete.

Over on Tahiti, Zeke was looking for new business opportunities for himself. He had sailed Hobie Cats in Hawaii and thought they would be popular in Tahiti. They are small, double-hulled crafts with a mast and sail in the middle, and are perfect for sailing in the lagoons. The island of Bora Bora was historically famous for its traditional, outrigger sailing canoes, and the people of Tahiti were ripe for a similar, yet faster and sleeker craft. Zeke arranged for a Hobie Cat to be delivered from Hawaii, and started sailing it around the island of Tahiti on weekends. He was noticed immediately. Before long, everyone wanted one, including Marlon. He wanted his guests to be able to sail in the lagoon at Tetiaroa. Although Hobies are fun, speedy, and have brightly colored sails, it was a potential problem for me. I wondered what the lagoon would look like with fast, colorful Hobie Cats zipping around. It seemed to me that they might detract from the peaceful, unobstructed views that I cherished and Marlon himself so loved. The Hobie dilemma established a quandary, as many other things would over time. "How does one live in undisturbed nature and still enjoy some of the advantages of modern technology?" Marlon and I pondered this question many times over the years. This particular time, we settled it by deciding we would have only one Hobie Cat on Tetiaroa — his. Zeke was delighted. He sold one to Marlon, and actually sailed it 30 miles across the open ocean, with captain Siki in a chase boat to make sure that if Zeke were to capsize, the sharks wouldn't eat him.

The ocean, as beautiful as it is, can be quite dangerous. One Sunday, Klaus, the mechanic, took Purea out sailing on Marlon's Hobie Cat. It was a beautiful day and no one thought much of it when they didn't return for lunch. As dusk approached, I started to feel slightly apprehensive, but the lagoon was calm and the weather fine. By dinnertime, when they still had not returned, the rest of us, at least the *popaas*, started to discuss what to do. Should we send out a search party? Where would we look? The lagoon was very big and it was dark. Do we do nothing until dawn? Could they have gone over the reef? In the ocean, anything could happen. Tiare Higgens, Michele's best friend, had recently disappeared in the Pacific. She was traveling with her boyfriend on a catamaran bound for New Zealand. They never arrived. We had held on to hope, but it was a catastrophe. Weeks, then months went by. They were never found. Michele was crushed; we were all saddened by the loss of our beautiful friend.

I decided we had to wait until sun-up, but I was edgy about the decision. That night there was a squall, which kicked up light rain and some pretty good winds. I knew that the Hobie, unless very well managed, could easily tip over, and would be hard to right in stormy seas. As the night wore on, I became so worried that I alerted the airport in Papeete in case an aerial search would be necessary in the morning. I spent a sleepless night waiting, but at sunrise, just as I was getting a search party ready to depart, we made out a sail on the horizon. Sure enough, it was the Hobie Cat. We wondered whether there were one or two people aboard. As the craft drew nearer, we realized that they were two, that they were wet, but that they were both very much OK. They told us they'd seen the squall approaching in the evening, had quickly beached the boat on one of the *motus*, turned it over to block the wind, and slept under the sail. From that day forward Purea brought Klaus little gifts with her from town, a *panier*, a basket of fruit, a little charm to wear around his neck, a bottle of his favorite wine. The rest, as they say in the South Pacific, is history!

The call of the 'Sirens' of the South Seas is powerful. After an eventful and adventurous year working on Tetiaroa, Klaus decided to leave us in order to move in with Purea in her grand house on the beach on Tahiti, where he could listen to the sirens' song forever.

An amusing side note to my various Tahitian escapades came about quite unexpectedly. The wife of a Chinese store owner and I liked to flirt with one another. It was innocent, or as innocent as these things can be. Her husband was much older, and very jealous of his glamorous young wife. As I'd come into the store to buy something, she would scurry into the rear isles where she was hidden from her husband and wait for me to round the corner. As I greeted her, she would turn her head toward me at the last instant of a polite kiss on the cheek, so that we'd instead be kissing on the mouth. Each time this happened, I was kind of startled, but a long way from displeased. I'd be lying if I said that I didn't look forward to it. I heard through the worker's "coconut radio" that one time she left home unannounced, and her husband promptly took a friend's fishing boat to Tetiaroa, looking for her. She was probably feeling 'fiu' and just disappeared for a few days. Be that as it may, she was not on Tetiaroa. That was a good thing, because I'm pretty sure he would have killed us both.

It was not the Polynesian women, beautiful and mysterious as they are, who lured me. For me, the atoll itself had become my siren. The attraction was physical as well as emotional. I was falling in love with Tetiaroa. It became, as time went on, like the love for a woman that does not let go, and that I would never get over.

The moon was my silent shining partner, as our world traveled through space. It glowed with an impossibly bright light, turning leaves into silver and gold, and illuminating the land, the lagoon and ocean beyond. It cast dark shadows, even at night — and did this only as a reflection of the sun. I found it astonishing!

The moon became my friend — with as many moods as a friend will have, from blue to flaming red. And like a good friend, it suddenly appears when all looks black. I could count on it to shed a sliver of light, and of hope that was always there — just temporarily blocked, out of sight.

Top
Forming beams for the round
reception building.

Bottom
Agnes helps out weaving niau.
The old copra drying shed in the background.

Tiare Higgins.

Photo by MD

Marlon's Hobie.

Michele and Dany Carlson plot an archaeological site.

Dr. Sinoto's school.

Top
Some students dig, others nap.

Bottom
Some of the tool artifacts found on Onetahi.

Dr. Sinoto's students excavating sites.
Sabrina and Poopie lend a hand.

Top
Michele at the burial site.

Bottom
Archaeological friendships.

The students had to build their own shelters out of native materials.

THE FINAL TOUCHES

We're Going to Crash!
Animal Farms

"Oh my god!" I thought, "We're going to crash!" I was on a little nine-passenger plane flying back to Tetiaroa from Papeete. The plane was mostly packed with produce in open boxes, strapped down to empty seats. The only other passengers were Dr. Sinoto and Michele. As soon as we touched the ground, I realized that the pilot had forgotten something crucial. I strained to hear the familiar sound of gears grinding, assuring me that the flaps that slow the plane down were being lowered. But I could hear nothing at all, and now we were racing along the runway way too fast. Michele, I noticed, was looking at the pilot in horror. He was frantically working the breaks. I braced myself for the worst as I saw a pile of rubble rapidly approaching. It stopped us cold — right at the water's edge. Suddenly, the plane tipped over on its nose, its tail in the air and the tip of a wing hitting the ground. There were vegetables and fruit all over the place, and I had a banana down my shirt collar. I stared over at the pilot, who wore an expression of shock, and then dismay. We both understood exactly what he hadn't done. He had not lowered the flaps! These pilots flew so often between Tahiti and Moorea and Tetiaroa that they were constantly landing and taking off. They probably landed their planes fifteen or sixteen times during a six-hour shift, and to them everything was automatic. Our pilot had obviously been distracted. Maybe Marlon had mooned the plane. He'd do that from time to time. I don't know. All I can attest to is that we ended up with the nose and one wing on the ground, all jumbled up inside the plane with melons rolling down the aisle — dazed but unharmed.

Marlon came dashing across the sand. He and a group of workmen pulled us through the door while the pilot remained inside, speechless. When the pilot finally emerged, Dr. Sinoto went up to him, bowed, and politely said "Thank you very much. Is this the way you always land?" Marlon, not to be outdone, offered Dr. Sinoto a glass of wine, and said, "Welcome to Tetiaroa."

The runway had only recently opened, and I could guess what lay ahead: the pilot would blame his blunder on something wrong with our runway. The plane looked OK, except for a twist in the wing, which we all knew could be a big problem. Airplane wings are constructed as a structural beam that can be bent, but if broken, cannot support a plane in flight. I had two hefty Tahitians grab the wing tips and push and pull up and down while the pilot and I looked for cracks in the fuselage. The wing was indeed bent, but seemed not to be broken. The pilot checked the propellers and both motors, and said he felt confident the plane would fly. He was nervous, but seemed eager to get out of there. He and I conferred with Marlon. The pilot told us he would start the ignition, drive down the runway, and, if everything felt right to him, he would take off low over the lagoon. He told us that if the plane proceeded to respond well to the controls, he would continue on to Tahiti, one-half hour away, but stay close to the water. If the plane was not responding well, he said he would try to turn it around and land again on the runway. If he couldn't turn around for some reason, he would have to splash into the lagoon. Marlon was all for calling the airport in Papeete to ask for help, but I knew that if we called, there would be an investigation and Tetiaroa's airstrip would be closed for some time. "Let's take a chance," I begged Marlon. "We'll know right away if the plane is airworthy. We'll notice if it doesn't fly, and then we'll call for help." The pilot really wanted to get going, and told Marlon it was his decision to make. Knowing that Air Tahiti in Papeete was going to ask what the hell had happened, and that the pilot was going to lie, I wanted to go with him in order to make sure they knew it was the pilot, not our runway, who was at fault. Marlon argued against my going, "Bernie you're crazy; you're going to get yourself fucking killed." But this time, I prevailed. Before anyone else got involved, the pilot and I jumped on the plane. He revved up the motors, turned the plane around, and started back down the runway. When we reached the end and turned again to take off, the pilot tested the flaps and the rudder and gunned the engines a couple of times. We looked at each other, ground our teeth, arched our eyebrows, and nodded: "OK." It was now or never. He gunned the motors again, let go of the brakes, and rolled down the runway, gaining speed as we neared the end. I have no idea what was in the pilot's head, but I was silently begging, "Come on plane, lift, come on, lift, lift, please, lift off!" At the last instant, the pilot eased up on the wheel and slowly up we went, over the lagoon. We both continued to hold our breath as the plane gradually made a big circle over the lagoon. He made an adjustment for the bent wing because holding the horizon wasn't easy. We made a gentle turn, held at 500 feet, and off we went over the ocean.

As we approached Tahiti, it suddenly disappeared behind thick clouds, and we had no choice but to go right through them. The pilot didn't want to climb or make any quick turns because of the damaged wing, so in we went, blindly. After what seemed like an eternity with nothing but white all around us, a mountain appeared directly ahead. We had to turn sharply, which put a lot of pressure on the wing. Terrified, I peered out the window expecting to see the wing fly off, but the plane held together. We had avoided catastrophe for the second time that afternoon. Finally, I could see Papeete and the airport. What a sight! The pilot radioed the tower to have the runway cleared for an emergency landing. After touchdown, he drove straight into a hangar. He parked the plane, got out, and headed immediately into the employee's bar, where he ordered a cognac. I was right behind him.

I had made a dangerous decision, but I knew I had to make it to protect our runway from the lies the pilot was sure to have told. The accident was determined a pilot error, and the guy was fired straightaway. I caught hell from Dora for risking my life, but I had saved the runway and the hotel construction from being shut down. Marlon thanked me, but not before saying, "Bernie, you're a god damn idiot."

Now that planes could land and take off from our airstrip, we were able to bring in large pieces of equipment and many more visitors. We not only replaced the generator we had lost on the reef, we brought in a second one as well. For the first time, we had electricity on Onetahi! That insurance policy sure had paid off, I thought. I quickly learned, however, that insurance companies are the same all over world, and in order to justify the claim, I had to prove that the original generator was indeed gone. "Show us the parts," they had said, so we had to fly in an insurance adjuster from Lloyds of London. We told him that the generator was still submerged off the reef, and that he would have to dive to see it for himself. "No way," he said, "I'm not doing any diving." So we had to build a makeshift raft, winch the sunken generator up out of the water, get it onto the raft, and haul it ashore. Johnny, on one of his visits, had found old seaplane pontoons on one of the *motus*. He was able to jerry-rig them together into a kind of motorized raft. So one day we set out with some workers to find and retrieve the Lister generator that had been left on the reef the night of the storm. The Tahitian's loved the distraction from their regular duties. Being in the lagoon and on the reef was fun, not work, and they always made the most of it. We all returned at the end of the day with a rusty old generator and a bundle of fish, lobsters, and clams. All of that to prove to the insurance adjuster that this was the specific generator we had bought in the first place by showing him the serial number and giving him the parts.

All this ended up costing us dearly. I had thought that I had made a really good deal. I had paid the $3,000 for the original generator and the $3,000 for the policy. Oh, how I wished now that I had bought a more expensive policy! It took one day to build the raft and one day plus six men to get the generator out of the water. On top of that I had to buy a new generator and fly it out to the island. A lesson learned at a high price.

Another piece of equipment that arrived from Papeete was a broyer machine I had bought to cut up palm fronds so they could be used in composting. It had a big, sharp, horizontal steel blade that turned as it was hauled behind a jeep. It was really made for cutting grass, but I had it modified to cut large leaves, palm fronds, and small twigs as well. Marlon loved his new toy. He would hitch it up to the bulldozer and run rough-shod through the jungle trying to make new roads. It didn't take too long before that poor broyer's blade got bent out of shape, stuck, and eventually broken beyond repair. We now had no simple way of cutting up the piles of leaves that had been stockpiled for mulch and composting, and the piles were getting larger and higher every day. I was not going to get another broyer for Marlon to play with, so I decided that composting would have to wait until construction was finished. Much to my disappointment, I would learn later that the composting project never got off the ground at all.

Marlon and I were still hoping that there was some way for us to make sure that people living on the island could support themselves in ways other than working at the hotel, conducting tours, or renting out facilities to scientists. Marlon brought Carl Hodges, the aquaculturist, back to Tetiaroa to help us consider our options for raising fish, animal life, or anything else that could be sold in town. Marlon, who had originally dismissed our early conversations about pearl farming, became immediately enthusiastic when he realized that it could be a source of income. What was to become enormous growth in the production of black pearls had just started. They were being sold across the globe, and Polynesia, where black pearls are found naturally, was beginning to commercialize its native treasure for the first time.

During the 1970s, the Japanese were the world's largest producers of cultivated, sparkling white pearls. They had also begun purchasing black pearls from Polynesia, grown and

Top
A Twin Otter, the largest plane that can land on Tetiaroa.

Bottom
The replacement generator arrives.

Getting the old generator out of the lagoon.

Moeata came along to join the fun.

cultivated on remote islands where the lagoon waters are clean and free of pollution. There was an increasing market for black pearls not only in Japan, but also in New York and Paris, and therefore a need for greater pearl production in Tahiti. The question for us was whether black pearl oysters would thrive in our lagoon. In order to find out, we sent for baby black pearl oysters from the Tuamotu Islands. The plan was for us to place the oysters in the coral of the reef, in various places where the nutrient-rich current was strongest. By monitoring the growth of the oysters, we could determine if the shells were producing the specific mother-of-pearl necessary for black pearl cultivation. Marlon approved a pilot program we called *mona mona*, meaning "very sweet." We hoped it would eventually become a commercial enterprise specializing in natural products from Tetiaroa. I assigned Michele and William, a native of the Cook Islands who had been on our construction crew, to head up the day-to-day operations.

Tetiaroa's lagoon had never belonged to Marlon. The lagoons and reefs of Polynesia belong to the government, and therefore to the Polynesian people. Accordingly, we had to request a special license from the government in order to open a pearl farm. Marlon, who hated bureaucracy, didn't think that we needed permission just to test whether or not black pearl oysters would grow in "our" lagoon. He was for going ahead without telling anyone. I was dubious, as I knew that everyone on the island would know what was going on and we would be caught. But Marlon said "fuck it, just do it," and so we did.

I mapped prospective sites for cultivation along the reef and then went about planting the young oysters without telling anyone. Michele and I took a canoe and headed out early one morning. I was in the steering position in back, with a bag of oysters in small nets, some reinforcing rods, a hammer and our masks, snorkels, and fins between my knees. The re-bars, when planted in the reef, were going to be used as markers at each test site location. Michele was in the bow, and I couldn't help being fascinated by the wind whipping her hair across her face, her body erect as she paddled with practiced strokes, three on one side, three on the other. I stopped paddling myself to admire her bronzed shoulders, and the tiny, thin delicate blond hair on her skin that sparkled like gold as each hair caught the sun with the movement of her arms. She had taken off her top, and her sinuous back, shifting with each stroke, was pure sculpture in motion. I was captivated. Her hips, emerging from her slim waist, flared out in an ogee curve. I was reminded of the famous Man Ray photograph of a violin superimposed on the back of a woman. My reverie was broken by the sound of crashing surf as we approached the reef. It was time to stop admiring her and to get to work. As I anchored the canoe, Michele slipped over the side and I handed her mask and fins. Off she went looking for appropriate corals on the reef. I followed with the bag of oysters, hammer, and re-bars. The water was clear, and the reef was full of brightly colored fish that scurried away or hid in the coral nooks as we approached. There were clams as big as a hand, their blue-green mouths wide open ready to be clamped shut at the slightest provocation. I wondered how we would ever find the oysters again in this underwater landscape, but trusted that the re-bar markers would stay put. The current and the tow of the reef water's ebb and flow made it impossible for us to remain in a fixed position. Thus it was not easy hammering the re-bars in after my mermaid partner had tucked the oysters, in their nets, in coral crevasses along the reef. Finally, after planting and marking a dozen sites, we swam leisurely back to our canoe, encountering reef sharks and even a young barracuda. I wished I had brought an underwater camera along, for more reasons than one.

We had already discarded the idea of fish farming due to the high cost of energy. Our lagoon, however, did have nesting grounds for green turtles. We knew that turtle meat was considered a delicacy and if they could be raised and sold in Papeete, turtles would provide work and profit for our village. But there were hurdles to overcome. The Pacific green turtle is a protected species, and they grew in the lagoon that belonged to the government. I contacted the South Pacific Commission, charged with the preservation of turtles, to ask them if turtles could be collected as they hatched in the sandy beaches. If we got them before birds got to them, we might be able to save quite a few. Roughly 90% of turtles are eaten as they scurry across the sand, trying to reach the lagoon. If we were able somehow to save 50% of the hatchlings, care for them until they were big enough to care for themselves, and let half go, would we be permitted to raise the remainder in a turtle farm? And would we be allowed to sell the ones we raised in the fish market in Papeete? Much to my astonishment, the answer was "yes." Reporting my findings to the authorities in Tahiti, I got a dubious bureaucratic OK because I had the paperwork!

Michele and William now had a second project. We didn't know anything about raising turtles, particularly with our minimum resources, or how long it would take to raise them to market size. We checked with turtle farms in the Caribbean and found that it was indeed possible. After researching the literature they sent us, it was decided to test the economics of the enterprise by raising 200 green turtles from hatchlings.

While awaiting the turtle hatching period, we turned our interest to another creature that was plentiful on the motus of Tetiaroa: *kaveos*, bright-blue coconut crabs. They grow to be very large, more than 2 feet across from claw to claw, and are so strong that they can actually crack a coconut in half with their claws. The government did not consider them an endangered species, although they were endangered indeed. They were hunted as a delicacy, and could be found only on the most remote islands. We knew they could be sold on the Papeete market for at least $25 each, as they were both rare and delicious. How much would it cost to raise them? Could they even be raised in captivity? How long do they live? What do they eat besides coconuts and how much do you feed them? The only way to find out was to experiment. We would try to raise *kaveos* as a third project, along with turtles and oysters.

One of the more fortunate aspects of these projects was that they didn't need employees with specialized skills, nor did they require any energy consuming technology. It was now clear that a new base camp would be necessary, away from the hotel and near the natural turtle hatching grounds. Michele and William found a suitable site on *motu* Tiaraunu, where they found evidence of many turtle nests. The *motu* was perfect for raising both turtles and *kaveos*. William made a clearing near the beach, constructed a fenced-in park for the *kaveos*, and set about finding some pregnant *kaveos*. Curiously, he knew how to identify them .

William had collected two dozen newborn *kaveos* that looked like tiny shrimp wiggling and scrambling about on the sand, searching for an empty shell to occupy. *Kaveos* are just like hermit crabs, vulnerable until they grow a hard carapace, or shell. It didn't take long for us to find out that our open park-like enclosure didn't work, even when the young were well fed on fresh coconut crumbs. They burrowed beneath the fence, attacked, and tried to eat each other. Even at a young age, they are carnivorous. This should not have come as a surprise to us, as we knew that full-grown *kaveos* eat rats. They catch them at the base of coconut trees just as the rats start to scamper up the trunk. In fact, that is where *kaveo* nests are found, in holes near the roots of coconut trees.

We made special individual cages out of strong wire mesh to prevent the crabs from fighting and attacking each other. Different sizes of empty shells had to be found for them to feel comfortable living in. Later, they needed trees to climb to strengthen their claws and extra sand so they could bury themselves to get away from the sun. We had to collect coconuts, split them, and break up the insides to feed the young. It was all very labor-intensive, and before we knew it, four people were operating the farm full time. The *kaveos* were very beautiful and, after a few months, they were as big as a human fist, but raising them to market size would take a few years and a lot of work. Much to our sorrow and frustration, the *kaveo* project had to be discontinued after six months. The project held too many unknowns and involved too much labor. We had learned a lot, however, and vowed to revisit the project in the future, when we'd have more resources.

Turtles, we discovered, created a whole other set of problems. Once rescued from the beach, half were let go into the lagoon and the other half were moved to tubs, with about a dozen or so per tub. The tubs had to be filled with fresh lagoon water every day. We had no pumps, and so we had to lug the water into the tubs. We fed the little turtles bits of fresh fish, which we had caught. Sometimes a tub would become contaminated, and all the turtles would die. We had to have plenty of tubs on hand, because as the little turtles grew, they needed more and more room. We bought larger tubs, which took longer to fill and were heavy to carry. It was a lot of work. As the turtles outgrew their tubs, we created a park in the lagoon for them. It was a wire mesh enclosure about 25 by 80 feet wide. The turtles seemed happy enough, but they had to be hand-fed because they were still not strong enough to swim against even a slight current inside the enclosure. We surmised that the tubs had been too small for them to develop the necessary strength in their flippers. We actually had to teach them how to swim by luring them with bits of fish tied to a string trailed in front of them. Talk about labor-intensive! Marlon was not to be dissuaded, however. He loved those little guys, and so we continued the project. Eventually the turtles learned to find their own food, chunks of shark that we threw into the park. By the end of 1975, after I was gone, they had grown to be about 6 inches across. We had invested a lot of time and energy, and it looked like we finally had a winner. Unfortunately though, in 1976 a whale of a storm created large waves in the lagoon that wiped out the turtle park. All the turtles escaped. The storm also wiped out the oyster site markers. I'm sure the oysters themselves came to no harm, but the storm ripped the spirit out of "Mona Mona," and regretfully, Marlon abandoned all three projects.

Giant coconut crabs (kaveos).

Top
Baby coconut crabs look like hermit crabs...

Bottom
but grow up like this.

Top
We raised kaveos in cages, because they attack each other.

Bottom
The start of our turtle farm.

Top
Michele tending our hatchlings.

Bottom
William and Michele check the buckets every day.

We kept a full-grown turtle in the turtle park to teach the young how to find food .

Top right
*This was as big as they got
before the storm hit.*

Bottom right
*Teaching baby turtles to feed themselves;
bits of shark meat hang from a string.*

Winds can be your best friend or your worst enemy. I rejoiced in the breeze that cooled the perspiration on my skin and brought the smell of oncoming rain, the breeze that billowed and fluttered a long cloth *pareu* not quite clinging to the hips of a lovely *vahine* sauntering down the beach. I also enjoyed the soft wind that kept mosquitoes at bay and played amusing, rippling games with schools of fish on the surface of the lagoon. The trade winds were my not-so-silent partner on the atoll. The sound of wind-driven, mesmerizing wavelets on the beach put me to contented sleep at night. But the ever-present wind that rustles palm leaves day and night, a pleasant sound at first, became a subconscious presence that after years left me yearning for quiet. I was sure it would eventually drive me nuts. Maybe it did.

Storms and squalls that came unexpectedly, often violent, made me thankful for shelter, and grateful that flapping tents didn't blow away or that roofs and walls didn't cave in. They were scary storms that made believers devout and agnostics searching for prayers. Fortunately these storms disappeared just as they had appeared. Hurricanes, mercifully rare in Tahiti, hurl coconuts like cannon balls, and if it were not for the reef, would swallow an atoll in their fury.

I longed for silence, or so I thought. The incessant roar of the surf was telling me that I was there, in a faraway place, at sea. And there was the rustle of the palm leaves, sometimes coming to me in a mad rush of awakening, but mostly hidden by my protective, active thoughts. They were there nonetheless, keeping me on edge. The constant lapping of the little lagoon waves on the sandy beach added to the symphony. On rare occasions at night, both wind and waves would stop. I would wake with a start. The silence was louder than sound, because the rustle and rippling had become a friendly reminder that all was well in my world: that day would always follow night; that the lagoon, a mere puddle on the surface of the sea, would be there in the morning for me to see. In the end, the sounds were telling me that I was welcome.

The hotel was close to completion. All the thatch-roofs had been finished and had already turned from their newly built brown to a more established silvery gray. Taken together, the buildings began to feel like a real village in a coconut grove. The land between buildings had been cleared, and low creeping vines and fresh green grasses were replacing the sandy soil. It was the negative spaces, the spaces between the buildings that I liked the most. The low roofs amongst the towering trees left room for views over the lagoon and over the reef. Patches of brilliant sky and sun-lit grass would come as a pleasant surprise as one walked about the site. I decided not to put any paths between the buildings, and to allow our visitors to roam at random, making visual discoveries as they went. My basic plan was to scatter the sleeping bungalows in the trees not far from the beach, while using the hotel's main building and outdoor bar as a central point of orientation. The circular bar was positioned on a white sandy beach, so as to allow views across the ever-changing turquoise and emerald-green lagoon all the way to the tiny *motus* in the distance. From the bar, the *motus* gave a sense of the atoll's size but also its limits. They somehow embraced the lagoon, and at the same time represented a very real separation from the world beyond.

The crescent-shaped main building housed a dining area at one end, a boutique at the other, and a lounge in the middle. I had built up the floor level to 3 feet above the natural grade, so that the low roof overhangs would provide much-needed shade, but would not cut off spectacular views all around. Roof overhangs were an important architectural element for light control. I was well aware that the quality of Tahitian light changes drastically depending on the time of day. The morning light over the lagoon was palpable: soft, warm, and glowing. It felt smooth and golden on my skin. The evening light was a glow of pinks and oranges with a flash of green just before sunset; it made my flesh look alive, healthy, and ruddy. At noon the light was too bright and blinding on the white sand and reflective waters; it swallowed up all the colors and cast harsh shadows. The building overhangs had to shield midday light, but also let the early morning and evening light in. They had to offer protection from the rain, because the windows, hinged awning affairs made of woven *niau*, were only closed during heavy, driving rains. I loved to watch water dripping off the thatch overhangs, the ribbons of drops resembling beads of pearls as each droplet caught the light on its decent.

Some of the bungalows, located in the trees away from the beach, had raised floors and balconies. As soon as the first one of these was completed, Marlon moved in. He quickly established himself there, seated in a large driftwood chair, his feet on the balcony railing, overlooking his very own private domain with satisfaction. He loved to just sit and watch. Once he told me, "It's the only place in the world were I can find peace. I can live in harmony with this little bit of the universe."

An inexplicable bond, inexplicable at least to me, had formed between Marlon and me. A bond strong yet elusive — based, I suppose, on trying to create reality out of the ether of a dream. I was a captive of the process, indulging myself in it, happy with it — at least most of the time. On the other hand, the dream itself was what counted for Marlon. It energized him. It was a dream that could give birth to other dreams, as the ocean gives never-ending birth to wave upon wave.

The wonderful thing about being on that island was that the reality in our minds had precious little resemblance to something tactile, concrete or alive, but it certainly kept us going. At times it seemed to me that Marlon enjoyed trying to make things come true by employing the sheer force of his will. Alas, an exercise in futility. He was good at making believe. He was an actor, after all. He could actually make himself believe the make-believe!

Marlon and I had become so close that there was little need for artifice between us. We talked, lying on our backs under the stars, engaged in meaningful, meaningless talk about women, as men are apt to do sometimes.

"I tell ya, Bern, she's got a great bod, but it's fucking stainless steel from her tits to her toes."

"Oh, you're so full of shit, Bud."

The electrical, sewage, and plumbing systems were progressing well. All wiring was installed underground. We made sure septic tanks and their leach lines were situated as far as possible from our water wells, and I was happy to find that tests of the well water met U.S. standards for drinking water. A small pump pumped the water from the wells into an enclosed cylinder. The compressed air in the cylinder then forced the water into a reservoir located high in the trees for gravity feed to various buildings. We bought low flush toilets (replacing my original order) and had huge clam shells brought in from the Philippines for sinks in the bungalows. We started testing wind energy with a windmill, and solar energy with photovoltaics. Everything was going swimmingly, except for one thing: we were constantly running out of money.

Financially, things were going badly, and not only on Tetiaroa. Dora was writing to me from Los Angeles, "I need money. I have to pay bills. They're piling up. Don't do this to me!" It was true. I had not been paid for months and wasn't able to send her a cent. I was not only juggling my financial affairs, but also Marlon's. I was ignoring Tarita's grocery bills as much as those of my wife. I paid some bills, but not others, borrowing from the bank and sending "please help" wires to Marlon's accountants in Beverly Hills. Things were getting critical. We were operating on bank credit. At one point, I had not paid the workers for a month, and was left in an uncomfortable quandary. I wanted to get the job done and I didn't want to stop, just pull out with the crew and all. It would have been next to impossible to get them back again. For me it was not, nor had it ever been, about money. My Tahitian crew would keep on working if I asked them to, for a while at least, but they had to be paid. Eventually Marlon would have to go back to work and I told him so. He initially resisted and left it up to his business mangers in Los Angeles to get me the funds to finish the job. They were going crazy trying to pay all of Marlon's bills. Zeke had let me overdraw about $100,000, but that was the limit. I was called to Papeete, and the bank manager gave me a rough time. I promised everyone on the crew they would be paid if they would just hang in there with me a little longer. On Tetiaroa, I had evidently built up enough good will as "Papa Bernard," and they were willing to go along with me.

Tahitians won't work just for money. A relationship has to be built up slowly. Authority derives from the kind of person you are as a leader, how you treat people, how considerate you are. Tahitians will work to help you because they like you or respect you. Taputuari's men knew him well and trusted him completely and would do extraordinarily dangerous things for him. I had lived and worked with most of the crew since they had disembarked on the reef, and we had experienced both rough times and happy fetes together. I respected them and they respected me. They trusted me. I recall a time in the early days, when we were preparing for the landing. I had gone out to Tetiaroa with one of Taputuari's men. We were alone for a full day at the old village checking on the rainwater collection cisterns. That evening, while waiting for Siki to return to pick us up by the old pier, we ran across a group of French military and their families having a picnic on the beach. After a little while, one of the officers approached and asked if I would like to join them for a drink. Noting that my Tahitian companion was definitely not invited, I politely refused. We waited on the beach for what turned out to be several hours, no more than 25 yards from the picnickers as they happily drank their wine and ate their meal. A story like that gets around. From the beginning, the Tahitians knew where I stood.

When things got too hectic at the construction site, I would escape. I'd sneak away by myself, find a canoe, and take off. I loved paddling across the lagoon all by myself in an outrigger canoe. There was little noise, just the dip and drip of my paddle in the clear deep water. I'd watch the ever-so-slight wave at the bow of the outrigger's wooden, white painted *ama* snake along its length until it disappeared on the turquoise surface. It was mesmerizing and soothing, and it placed me in a world of calm and inward contemplation. At times, with a burst of energy and swift, strong strokes, I'd force the canoe forward and let it glide to a stop. It released pent-up energy. The muscles of my back, shoulders and arms felt relieved. It also allowed me to reflect on how lucky I was to have these extraordinary experiences. Rejuvenated, I'd return to work.

*I loved to go out by myself in a canoe
with an outrigger ama.*

An overcast sunset.

Onetahi is starting to look park-like and habitable.

Finishing an awning window.

View from Marlon's bungalow.

Top
Marlon's bungalow.

Bottom
Nape covering a construction joint.

Ceiling of Marlon's hut.

Top
An enclosed pump cylinder.

Bottom left
A water reservoir in the trees.

Bottom right
Plumbing goes in.

Top left
Our radio tower, and our wind power testing tower.

Top right
Testing photovoltaics for solar power.

Bottom
A sink made from a shell.

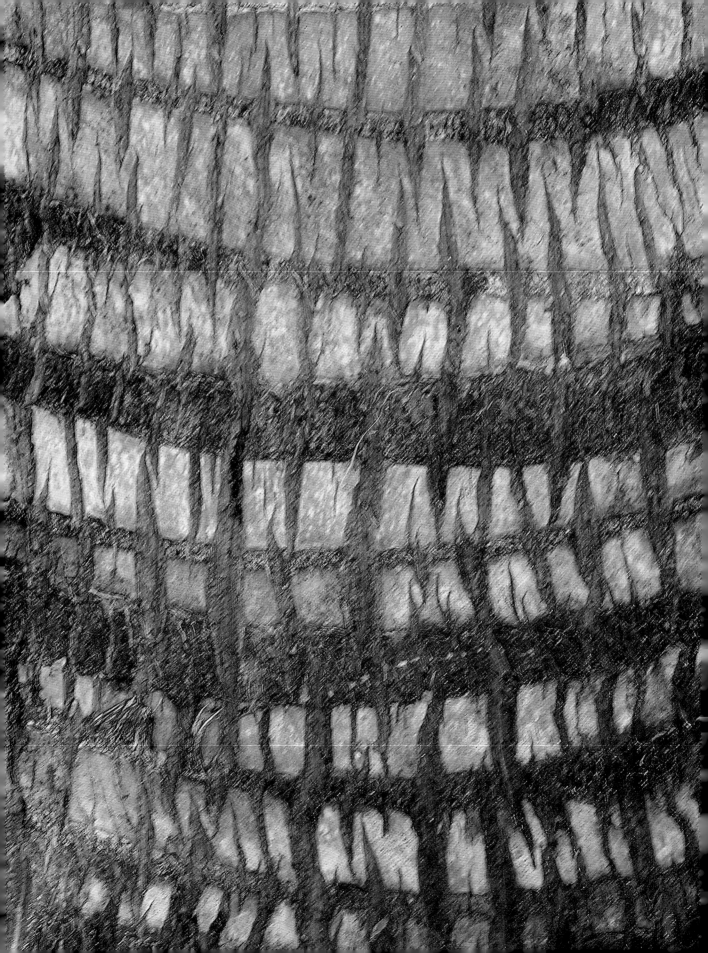

Late Summer 1973

THE WALTZ IS OVER

Shuffling Girlfriends
Oscar Night

In the spring of 1973, I got a call from Brown Kraft, Marlon's business managers, asking me to attend a meeting at Marlon's home in Beverly Hills. I asked Ron in my Los Angeles office to come to Tetiaroa to take my place there and make sure the workers didn't feel abandoned. Dora, Sabrina, and I left Tetiaroa, not knowing what lay ahead. I was apprehensive, but I also knew I was not replaceable, and that they knew that I knew that I was not replaceable. There had not been any problems between myself, Marlon, and Brown Kraft; the big question was, would they be able to come up with the funds to finish the job? I dressed for the occasion and put on my best herringbone Harris tweed suit, blue button-down oxford shirt, and striped tie. When I arrived at the Beverly Hills house, both Norty Brown and the accountant, George Pakkala, were already there. I knew that this was serious business, because Marlon, for once, was sitting in the living room, not lying on his bed. I went up to him and kissed him on both cheeks, as is the custom in Tahiti. He was a bit put off by the kiss under the circumstances, and the others seemed a bit surprised, but the moment passed quickly as a new person entered the room. He was introduced as Roger, a developer who had successfully built apartment houses in the state of Washington. Norty and George had greeted me warmly. We had met many times. They had come to Tetiaroa and seen my work, and I had been sending them monthly progress reports and financial statements since Marlon first hired me. I felt slightly pressured by the presence of a developer, but I confidently outlined my plans for the completion of the project. Construction of the hotel still had to be finished before it could be opened. I provided them with estimates for the remaining work, but could not and would not supply fixed dates or costs. My experience over the past years told me that I could not guarantee anything. I described many of the difficulties we had weathered — storms, lack of spare parts, delays, holidays and their aftermath. Then, finally, I reminded them that the workers had not been paid in a month. I told them that the Bank of Tahiti was being helpful, but would not be extending any more credit. I promised Marlon that I would stick it out for as long as it took, but if the workers were not paid and left, it would take months to get them back, if ever. Marlon stated his determination to finish the project on Tetiaroa, and in the end, Norty agreed to send the necessary funds to Tahiti as soon as possible. They accepted my estimates, but told me that Roger would be in charge of finances from then on. He would most likely also run the hotel. I was surprised to hear that, but quite relieved to have the financial responsibilities lifted from my shoulders, and content that we had averted yet another disaster. Roger was a typical numbers man with no outward warmth, no sense of humor, not even a ready smile. I was curious as to how a *popaa* with no experience in the hotel business could take on such a project. How would somebody who had never been to Tahiti and couldn't speak French, let alone Tahitian, run a small hotel on an atoll in the middle of the Pacific? The thought boggled my mind. I wondered where Marlon had found him and why he thought Roger could do the job. Under the circumstances, it didn't seem appropriate to ask, and so I didn't. I did, however, try to enumerate some of the difficulties that Roger would encounter, not the least of which was to master a complete change in culture and work ethic. When I mentioned the working conditions, he seemed unimpressed. That worried me. But I was happy because I knew I could finish my part of the project.

Upon my return to Tetiaroa, the crew was duly paid and went back to work. I was hailed as a hero by the Tahitians, and by Zeke, who had really put his reputation on the line for me at the bank.

Dora stayed in Los Angeles to finalize her work on the graphics for the hotel brochures, stationary, logo, and silk screens for the bed sheets. Marlon approved all her designs. He was delighted with the colorful silk screens and particularly fond of the logo. That logo, a baby coconut crab emerging from a turreted seashell, was meant to be symbolic of his attempt to protect nature on the atoll. It was exactly what he was looking for. He wanted the logo to represent his legacy: the protection of the atoll as he had promised Mrs. Duran and her daughter. The logo was used until the day he died.

Alice showed up with Marlon soon after my return from L.A. Life and work on the atoll resumed with a new sense of purpose. Tarita was busy with the construction of her new house on the front lawn in Punaauia and Marlon started to receive guests on Onetahi once again. Alan Grinnell dropped in for a visit en route to New Guinea. Quincy Jones stayed for a week. Marlon's sister Jocelyn was with us for a while, as were some old chums from Nebraska and their teenage kids. They all knew Marlon as "Bud," not as a movie star. I was taken by their natural, unaffected Midwestern ways. Agnes, as lovely as ever, and full of gaiety and laughter, came back and became our unofficial hostess. It was very much like the old days around the campsite: great food and conversation at the dinner table. As for Marlon, he was eager to engage in his usual mischief.

One night Alan told us that there was a time in Los Angeles when Marlon called him in the midst of a dinner party to ask him if urine was safe to drink! When Alan replied, "Yes, but why do you ask?" Marlon explained that he was with a bunch of girls at his house on Mulholland Drive and they were all discussing how they would survive on a deserted island. A couple of people had mentioned drinking their own urine and Marlon suggested they see what it would be like. They had all peed in a pot, had boiled the result, just to be safe, and it had turned bright blue. Marlon asked Alan, "Is it OK to drink bright-blue urine?" Alan quickly surmised they had boiled the urine in a copper pot, and determined it would not hurt them. "Go ahead, help yourselves." Marlon was epileptic with laughter as Alan told the story.

Not to be outdone, Marlon himself told a story about the 'green man.' He said that during the filming of *One Eyed Jacks* in the Arizona desert, the green man kept disappearing. He said the green man was the person who was supposed to provide green plants for a shot that needed foliage. This particular green man was apt to go off looking for green leaves in the desert, and having not found any, would simply doze off behind a rock somewhere. One time Marlon, who was also directing the movie, got so annoyed waiting for the green man that he picked up a shovel and went out to find him, shouting: "I'm going to wallop that son of a bitch and teach him a lesson for not ever being here when we need him." After unsuccessfully searching for a him in the hot sun, Marlon sat down on a rock. Catching a movement behind a nearby bush, he knew he had found him, and silently crept up behind the bush. Carefully peering through the leaves Marlon discovered that it was indeed the green man, but that he was not sleeping.

Top
*The first brochure, designed
by Honeya Barth.*

Bottom
*The Tetiaroa stationery, designed
by Dora.*

He was, as Marlon told it, "taking a crap." Marlon snuck back, got his shovel, returned to the place behind the bush, and waited for the green man to finish what he was doing. Marlon then gingerly slid the shovel under the turd, removing it. The green man, looking back with satisfaction while hitching up his pants past his knees, did a double take when he could not see the fruits of his labor. "With complete surprise," Marlon laughed, "he looked again, then all around and finally up in the air, even in the sky!" Marlon practically fell off the bench in hysterics as he told us the story. He would never have made a good straight man. Telling a funny story with a poker face was impossible for him, particularly when it was about himself.

New guests arrived on Onetahi around that time: young ladies, each more exquisite, alluring, and more exotic than the last. Marlon introduced the first as "a writer who was helping him with a book." She spent a lot of time in Marlon's hut, no doubt assisting him with "writing." A few days later, another lovely girl arrived. This one was there to "help decorate the bungalows," beginning, of course, with Marlon's. Alice, forever protecting Marlon, took the first girl, "the writer," and showed her the *motus* and the bird islands, but it soon became complicated keeping her away at night. Both girls were under the impression that she, not the other, was Marlon's girlfriend. After a few days of hilarious attempts at trying to hide one girl from the other, Alice had had enough of Marlon's games. She got ready to leave the island, abandoning Marlon to his own well-deserved fate in the hands of two lovers. As Alice waited by the runway for a plane to disgorge its passengers, Marlon begged and pleaded with her not to leave. Then out of the plane came yet another girlfriend! Disgusted, Alice boarded the plane and closed the door behind her. The pilot revved the engines and started to roll away as Marlon re-opened the door, yelling above the roar of the motors "Alice, don't leave me now!" Furious, the pilot turned and screamed: "Shut the door! Now!" Marlon, who was running alongside finally had to let go, and Alice grabbed the door from inside shouting for the pilot to keep going! The pilot did just that, and Marlon was alone with his harem.

The three women, each originally led to believe that she had been invited to spend the time of her life on a deserted island in the middle of the Pacific alone with Marlon Brando, finally caught on. The day after Alice fled, the first girl left for Papeete, infuriated. Alice, still in Papeete, was the one who had to find her a hotel room. It was a holiday weekend, and all hotels were booked. Alice had no choice but to book the girl in her own hotel. A day later, Alice got a call from the airport. The two other women were asking for her, because they needed hotel rooms as well. Alice called around, but could not find any more rooms. In desperation, she put them all together in the one room at her hotel. Alice told me that at first they couldn't stand each other. First one, then the other two, went to the bar to get away from each other, but they all ended up swapping stories, laughing at themselves. Meanwhile, Christian and Miko also got on a plane and showed up at the hotel. The manager called

Alice to say that there were two young boys buying everyone drinks at the bar and charging it to Mr. Brando. Alice couldn't believe her ears. She got the boys, half drunk, into her room immediately, and as soon as she could, she got the girls on a plane and out of the country. She wanted to leave on the next plane herself, but ever loyal, she didn't.

That year, Marlon was nominated for an Oscar for his performance in *The Godfather*. I happened to be in Los Angeles at the time. Naturally, I was hoping that he would win Best Actor, but even more than that, I couldn't wait to hear what he would say if he did win. Dora and I watched the TV broadcast at home on March 27, 1973 and when Marlon's name was announced, there was a terrific roar of applause. After a moment, we, along with the rest of the world, were surprised to watch an American-Indian woman in a buckskin dress and long braided hair stride up to the mic. As the applause died, she held up her hand signaling the host to stop, as he was preparing to hand her Marlon's golden statue. She explained that she was an Apache Indian representing Marlon Brando, who had sent a message that he could not accept the award. Despite gasps of shock throughout the audience, she went on to say that Marlon was respectfully refusing the Oscar because of the film industry's treatment of American Indians over the years. She thanked the Academy on behalf of Marlon and read from a prepared statement: "I would have been here myself tonight, but I thought I could do more good at Wounded Knee." At first the audience fell silent, but then, murmurs of disapproval grew ever louder. "Oh no..." Evidently, the Academy dislikes surprises and unscripted speeches.

From February 27 to May 8, 1973, activists from the American Indian Movement (AIM) took over the trading post and other buildings at Wounded Knee to commemorate the 1890 Indian massacre by the U.S. Army. Marlon's friends Russell Means and Dennis Banks, among others, were demanding the reexamination of various U.S. Indian treaties, as well as an investigation of activities of the Bureau of Indian Affairs (BIA). In the end, the activists were surrounded by FBI and army troops who shot and killed two people and wounded many more before the demonstration was over. As it turned out, Marlon never did go to Wounded Knee, and I never found out why.

The morning after the Oscars, I went up to Marlon's house and found Alice and Blanche having coffee in the kitchen with a very attractive Indian woman, whom I immediately recognized as the woman who had represented Marlon the night before. I told her how much I had admired her and her eloquence. She responded that "she had a good coach." She said that had it not been for the fact that she and Alice arrived at the awards ceremony at the very last minute, she would have had time to get nervous. She explained that Marlon had been writing out his statement, in long-hand, on a yellow legal pad while sitting in bed when the ceremonies started, and that Alice, waiting to type it up, had finally torn the pad out of his hands and typed it as Marlon dictated the last sentences. All the while, a driver had been waiting in the driveway to take them to the theatre, where she and Alice had practically had to sneak in. They had proper invitations and tickets, but the ushers had instructions not to let anyone in after the ceremony had started. Alice insisted on talking to the producer, who only relented because they represented Marlon. They had just taken their seats when Marlon's name was announced as the winner for *The Godfather*. Again, Alice had saved the day. Apparently Marlon had left early in the morning with his old friend Christian Marquand and no one really knew where they were going. I had to wait until I saw him again on Tetiaroa to thank him for the wonderful thing I thought he had done in recognizing Hollywood's false portrayal of American Indians. Marlon didn't want to talk about it.

Marlon continued to ban pesticides, herbicides, or fertilizers on the island, and despite our very best intentions, it was still difficult to keep Onetahi free from pests. We succeeded in getting rid of the mosquitoes at the base camp by keeping everything as clean as could be. We policed the grounds every day to make sure that there were no breeding grounds. Containers were not to be left open ever, particularly not after a rainfall. We quickly disposed of any open coconuts that rats or *kaveos* had nibbled through. Plants with open central axels that could collect rainwater were not allowed near the camp. To discourage flies, we covered our garbage cans and didn't leave any food or refuse around, especially not after eating fish. We also fell into the habit of scaling and gutting fish on the beach, where the remains would be washed away. We made sure that all coconut trees around the camp were banded against rats and that the legs of the kitchen equipment were set in shells filled with kerosene to keep ants and other crawlers out of our provisions. Airplanes coming in to Tetiaroa were supposed to be sprayed with insecticides before take-off and a good deal of the time these precautions, while not perfect, worked well. Well, sort of well.

Sabrina came back to Los Angeles with us during the time of the Oscars. She needed to see her doctor because of scabs on her legs that were not healing. The doctor, who had been in the South Pacific during World War II, recognized the symptoms at once. It was a case of "yaws," something he hadn't seen in thirty years, and never in Los Angeles. He told us that the disease was brought about by fly larvae living in festering sores, but that it had been eradicated in the United States years ago. Dora was horrified and Sabrina did not return to Tetiaroa for several years.

Top
Gilbert Letty, Zeke, and little Purea.

Bottom
Tea with her daughter Marau.

Photo by MR

Photo by MR

Top
Me, a friend, Tatua, Dolly, Kavika, Purea, and Zeke.

Bottom
Dolly, me, Tetua.

Top
Framing the communal hut. The span of the roof trusses and rafters was dependent on available trees.

Bottom
The communal hut.

I, of course, did go back. Later that spring, as I was walking to the construction site across our new grass runway one morning, I noticed that there was a patch of grass, perhaps a square yard large, that was practically bare. Looking closer, I could find nothing amiss with the naked eye. On the way back to my tent at noon, I noticed that the patch had become larger, so I got down on my hands and knees and, to my surprise, found little green caterpillars, the type one might see on lettuce leaves. Some lettuce or other vegetable had evidently been dropped on the runway while a plane was unloading, for I had found no indication of caterpillars on the island before that day. How could we get rid of them? I didn't want to use insecticides because the water table was only 2 feet below the runway. I hoped that birds would find them and finish them off before too much damage was done to the grass. In the meantime, the only thing to do was to stomp on them and crush them. Luckily, the grassy runway was bordered on both sides by 50 feet of white sand. The caterpillars would not cross the sand, which meant we only had to treat an area approximately 60 by 2,000 feet long! Sounded doable, but the critters were eating and multiplying faster than we could stomp them out, and they apparently had no natural enemies. Birds, tupas, and crabs completely ignored them. It was a losing battle, and we lost it in a week. The caterpillars finally disappeared because they ran out of food. They had eaten up the runway.

Dr. Sinoto came back for his annual archaeological dig, and the island was full of activity yet again. Thibault, the bird expert, was back counting new hatchlings. Marlon loved that I had arranged for some woodworking students from Tahiti to come to Tetiaroa to make furniture for the hotel. In Papeete, the students were using wood imported from the States and Australia to make furniture by copying designs found in Europe. I encouraged them to use lumber indigenous to the islands, and to make furniture of their own designs. Not only did I want the Tetiaroa furnishings to be unique and made of local materials, but I wanted the students to develop their own ideas and carry them through. I'm happy to report that the experiment proved a great success: the students not only learned a lot, but created chairs and tables that were used in the hotel dining room until the hotel closed in 2004. The pieces were a bit on the heavy side (you could hardly lift them) as they were made of ironwood, but they were well made, comfortable and certainly unusual.

Marlon left for New York in the early summer to do an interview with Dick Cavett, the television personality known for his liberal politics. Ivan and I were hoping that Marlon would mention Tetiaroa and our soon-to-be-opened hotel. That would have been fantastic publicity for us. We were disappointed that he chose not to, but as he explained to us when he got back, it was more important for him to discuss the plight of the American Indian. When I asked him about a bandage on his hand, he explained that he had broken it socking a photographer who was pointing a camera in his face. His hand had become infected, and I

Top
My private swimming pool.

Bottom
Tetiaroa's moods—night and day.

could tell that he was still mad at the photographer. It made me wonder what would happen if visitors to the hotel tried to get a snapshot of him. Would we have to ban photography, confiscate cameras when Marlon was around? It was a potential problem that would have to be resolved lest Marlon punch anybody else. Ultimately, we ended up limiting access to the atoll during the times Marlon was there. We only allowed his friends and locals on Tetiaroa, people who'd be unimpressed by the famous actor. As it turned out, the strategy worked well.

As the project was nearing completion, more and more of Marlon's friends came to visit. Connie Hall showed up to check out our garbage disposal system and composting methods. He was interested in using similar methods on his as yet uninhabited *motu* just off the southern coast of Tahiti. He also wanted to know what we were doing about rats. We told him that we were simply keeping the island as free as possible from open coconuts and as clean as could be. He responded with a better idea. "You take a 50-gallon drum, remove the top, and bury it with some open coconuts in the bottom. Some rats will fall in, attracted by the food, and won't be able to get out. To avoid starving, they will eat each other. More rats will fall in until all the rats on the island will have eaten each other except the last one, which will be bigger and stronger than all the others. Then, you just club the fucker to death." Marlon came back with a better idea: "You take that last fat rat and send him to Hollywood where he becomes the head of a studio. *Then* you club him to death." The two of them were always teasing each other about who could live the longest on a *motu* without any outside help.

"Without women," Marlon would add.
"How about with one woman?" Connie would ask.
"No!"
"How about with a teenage girl?"
"That depends."
"I thought you said 'no women.'"
"Well, a woman is not a girl."
"That depends."

On and on it would go till they were rolling on the sand in laughter.

When Ivan contacted the authorities about a license for the hotel, he discovered that we had never had building permits for any of the buildings. I had received a permit for the private airstrip and an approval for the general plan at the initial location, but had not applied for actual building permits. I had naively thought that since we were on a private island far from Tahiti, and were building out of native materials in a traditional Polynesian manner, we didn't need to have building permits. Ivan found that, in fact, Tetiaroa is officially considered

Inside a bungalow.

part of the community of Arue, which is located on Tahiti, 30 miles away. That was news to me. In fact, building permits would have been difficult to get since I was designing the buildings as I went along, and for the most part without any engineering plans. Without proper plans I would never have gotten a permit, even if I had applied for them. I had had no contact with authorities except when we were working on the runway. I had been building my own world, my way, and illegally.

"I've got the answer to this permit problem," Marlon exclaimed. "We'll invite the governor out here. I'll sweet-talk him."

So it was that one day the governor arrived by plane, dressed in his splendid white French uniform. We had made very special preparations for him. A table and three chairs had been set out on the beach overlooking the lagoon, with their backs to the construction site. The table was covered with a bright red *pareu*, and fragrant *tiare Tahiti* blossoms had been placed on a delicate oyster shell in the middle. Reiko had made three lovely goblets from green glass wine bottles. The chairs, consisting of a sail cloth slung from a frame made of weathered driftwood, were very comfortable and set firmly in the sand so that they couldn't be moved. The setting was rustic yet also elegant, comfortable, and typically Polynesian. Most importantly, we were served chilled champagne by a gorgeous, tall, barefooted model from Trinidad, dressed in a tiny *pareu* with a wreath of leaves modestly covering her breasts. There was no way this French governor could possibly concentrate on the construction behind him. The model was a friend of Marlon's, who just happened to be visiting Tetiaroa at the time, and was willingly pressed into service. Marlon, the governor, and I conversed in French about the unbelievable splendor of the atoll, its bountiful bird and aquatic life. Marlon could be most charming and solicitous, and that day he was at his best. When the governor brought up acting and asked Marlon who he thought was the best actor in the world, Marlon pondered for a moment. "Sir Lawrence Olivier, when it comes to the classical theatre." Then, after a brief pause, he added, "But as a modern actor, I have to say, I am." Later in the conversation, when Marlon asked the governor how he felt about being posted outside of France, the governor, seemingly surprised, thought for a minute, smiled, and replied, "But Marlon," pointing at the view, "I am in France." A French version of "gotcha!"

We never did get building permits, but Ivan got the hotel license anyway.

Top left
Kahia truss and palm leaf weave.

Bottom left
Looking for coconuts.

Right
View from the bar.

We built with natural material found on the atoll.

Top
The hotel lobby.

Bottom left
The moon, my friend.

Bottom right
Restroom for day tours.

Top
Tea seated at the bar.

Bottom
Hotel Tetiaroa reception.

Roger, the new hotel manager I'd met in Los Angeles, arrived on the island just as we were completing the final touches on the hotel. There was still a long slate of small things to do, but the punch list was getting shorter by the day. As Roger wanted to take over more of Ivan's duties in preparation for the hotel's grand opening, it became clear that Ivan had to go. I felt terrible about it, but there was nothing I could do. When I told Marlon about my concerns, he just replied: "Bernie, just give Roger a chance." For the first time, Marlon had made a decision about Tetiaroa without me, and I felt he had made a big mistake. Ivan had done a really fine job, but the hotel would have to open without him.

My somber mood probably gave everything away. It was clear to anybody who'd care to see that a complete regime change was about to take place. Even the Tahitian workers, particularly the ones who had been there from the start, knew just what was going on: Roger was taking over and they were not too happy about it. I, on the other hand, was naïve. I still thought of Tetiaroa as my project, and looked at Roger as somebody here to help me finish it. It had been me who started this; it had been me who had been living with it. "Papa Bernard" had become part of my identity, and I would not let Roger take that away.

But some things in life are simply out of anyone's control. My attention was fixed on getting the job done, and Roger and his new regime was interfering with my work. Roger didn't speak any French or Tahitian, and so I found myself translating for him all the time. There was undoubtedly some subconscious jealousy, and even unspoken hostility on both our parts. We were both polite to each other, and there was no outward friction, but the crew felt it nonetheless. They didn't take to Roger at all. Eventually, personalities clashed and he hired his own people to translate for him. Suddenly nothing, rather than everything, went through me. Roger was at the helm, and I had no choice but to help him. The project began to suffer. I told Marlon that I would finish the job nonetheless, and stay until the hotel was to open in August. I was so looking forward to that day. After all, this was what I had worked for and lived towards for such a long time. But in mid-July, Marlon, who was traveling often then, sent me a letter. It was hand-written on Pan Am stationary.

Dear Bernie,

The winds of change flew out of Roger's mouth this morning. He said, after he heard that I persuaded you to stay, that it was, in short you or him. I couldn't talk him out of it. I don't know a second position to take. However it's not the end of the waltz. I'm going to further discuss it with him in California. I think he might be less intractable. I'll let you know from there.

Love, Marlon

For me, the music stopped right then and there. The waltz *was* over. I packed my bags, took my files, burned my tent, thanked and hugged the Tahitian crew, and kissed everyone *"na na,"* goodbye.

Then, as I flew low over the lagoon I had come to know so well, I could feel the rhythmic push and pull of the waves on the coral reef just below. On that first day, they had pushed me away, and then pulled me back to stay for several happy years. I knew in my wounded heart that they would pull me back again some day.

The dining room of the communal hut.

Goodbye Tetiaroa.

Dear Bernie,

                The winds of change
blew out of Rogers mouth this morning.
He said, after he heard that I persuaded you to stay, that it was, in short
you or him. I couldn't talk him out
of it. I don't have a second position
to take. However it's not the end
of the waltz I'm going to further
discuss it with him in california
I think he might be less intractable
All let you know from there
                Love, Marlon

POSTSCRIPT

Ten Years Later

In 1983, a once-in-a-lifetime hurricane destroyed many of the main structures and some of the sleeping huts along the beach on Onetahi. It turned out that I had been right when I explained to Marlon years before that the hotel site he chose was too vulnerable to the elements. The black film on the sand should have been my clue: it pointed to salt deposits from previous saltwater inundations. The northern tip of Onetahi formed the funnel between Onetahi and the motu directly to its north. Because of the prevailing winds, the lagoon emptied between the two small islands, which caused a swift current. During heavy storms, this current would overflow and erode the northern tip of Onetahi, leaving a layer of salt and exposing the roots of trees on the shore. The Tahitian workers had said nothing when we changed the hotel site. They probably laughed amongst themselves: "Let the popaas learn for themselves."

When I heard of the hurricane, I was concerned and called the administrative office in Papeete. They told me that the atoll had been evacuated in time, and that no one was hurt, but that the hotel had been badly damaged. I felt bad, but vindicated at the same time. I should have insisted and kept up my initial opposition to the hotel site Marlon had wanted. Deep down inside, however, I knew that Marlon had made up his mind, and, Marlon being Marlon, my opposition would not have made any difference. It even would not have made a difference had I gone through with my threat and quit. He would have found someone else to build the buildings right where he wanted them to be built. I still feel that staying was the right thing to do. Marlon and I had shared a vision for the future of the atoll. He was, at times, difficult to work with, but I had started the project and believed in our goals, and was not about to abandon them, or him, at least willingly.

When I left, I left because Marlon did not leave me a choice. I returned to Los Angeles before the hotel opened, and I was dispirited. It was an abrupt ending to an adventure of a lifetime. Looking back, I know it was inevitable. There had been too much disagreement between myself and the new manager of the hotel. Marlon had to allow him some freedom to make decisions for himself. I was not going to stay beyond the completion of the hotel, Roger was. So when early disagreements surfaced, I had to go. I had been with Marlon so much for so long, living in a tent on a beach, following a dream. It had been nearly three years. It was hard to give it up. I was proud of what I had accomplished: a difficult project in a difficult location with a client and a shared vision. I would have liked nothing more than to be the one to hand the keys of the hotel over to Marlon. However, my mandate had never been to run the project after construction was completed.

Roger, a decent and capable fellow, did finish the hotel. Other popaas, however well-meaning, were never able to manage the hotel or its Tahitian staff for any meaningful length of time. In fact, two months after I left, the workers at the hotel went on strike and left the island. The dispute was eventually resolved, but it was hard to find adequate management after that. It was also hard to find workers who could be self-supporting in the way Marlon and I had originally envisioned. The hotel staff did not have any other work on the atoll, because Marlon had not managed to set up a truly self-sustaining village. Marlon had toyed with the idea of permitting employees with ten years of service to build their own houses on the atoll, thereby promoting self-sufficiency, schools, and community. But allowing workers to build their own houses would have meant relinquishing some control to them, and so Marlon shied away from this idea. Alice, who knew Marlon better than anyone, told me that Marlon loved Tetiaroa more than he loved any woman. Perhaps that was the reason he could not let go and allow others ownership of anything on the atoll. With one exception: he offered me the chance to build a house for myself and my family. I never did because when I had the time, I didn't have the money, and when I had the money, I didn't have the time. Besides, I didn't really need a house there. I could visit the atoll–and Marlon–any time I wished. Over the years, I did visit many times, often when Marlon was there. Marlon lived there happily until tragedy struck his family in 1990 when his son Christian killed his daughter Cheyenne's boyfriend, and Cheyenne committed suicide. Heartbroken, Marlon never went back to Tahiti or to Tetiaroa. Finally, he asked Tarita to take charge of the hotel, which she did until his death in 2004.

Did the vision we shared come true? Did we build a self-sustaining community based on aquacultue and nutricultue? Unfortunately not. On the other hand, did we protect the ecological system, the lagoon, the birds, turtles, and reefs? Were the archaeological sites preserved? Was the atoll open to scientists and students, writers, musicians, and particularly, the Polynesian people? Was the general public able to enjoy the peace, beauty, and exquisite solitude of Tetiaroa? The answer, I believe, is a definite yes. Cynthia Garbutt, Marlon's long-time Tetiaroa receptionist, once told me that by far the greatest number of guests were local Tahitians who loved to bring their children to the atoll to show them what life had been like before the automobile and the ravages of pollution had changed Tahiti. Not all things worked out as planned. On one of my later visits to Tahiti, I met a doctor and his wife who spent the weekend on Tetiaroa whenever they could. He made me laugh when he told me that Tetiaroa offered a wonderful respite from Papeete, but that every time he went he had to remember to bring a wrench and screwdriver with him to fix the toilet and shower in their bungalow.

I have kept in contact with many of the people I was fortunate enough to meet during my years working on Tetiaroa. Claude Girard, Marlon's attorney, who lent me his boat for that first survey trip, had me design his home in the hills above Papeete. He still lives there today. Conrad Hall became a cherished friend, and I will always think fondly of him and our days together on his little motu off of Tahiti. I was fortunate to get Tumata Robinson a role in the movie Overboard, *and I still enjoy seeing her in Tahiti and in Los Angeles. I count Paul and Jenny Faugerat among my dear friends. I have stayed at their mountain guesthouse many times during my visits in Tahiti. I continued to see Michele Darr while she was caretaker of the Malcolm Forbes' property on Tahiti Iti, but after that, we lost touch. I visit with Jean Shelsher in her painting studio on Moorea, and Agnes, whenever I can. Tea, her children and grandchildren, and her mother Purea, are my Tahitian family. I visit them often. Johnny married Moeata, his girlfriend from Tetiaroa days, and fled to the Gambiers. Alice Marchak interceded many times with Marlon on my behalf, for which I thank her. We remain good friends and we keep in touch regularly.*

Sadly, Dora and I divorced in 1980. She has become a celebrated artist and ceramist, and has had major exhibits in museums in Los Angeles, Washington, D.C., and Nagoya, Japan. In 1977, she had the honor of being commissioned to produce a dinnerware set for the Carter White House.

In 2002, Tarita invited Tea and me to Tetiaroa. When we arrived, Agnes was waiting for us at the runway. I hadn't seen her for many years. She was still all smiles, full of gaiety and laughter as she introduced us to a distinguished gentleman about my age, in his early seventies.

We learned that he had visited Tahiti as a young man, met Agnes, and that they had fallen in love. When he had had to leave Tahiti, he promised to come back . Some forty years later, after having had a family in Denmark, making a fortune, and living in a castle, he made good on his promise. He returned to Agnes, and they were clearly still in love. Like the magnetism of tides on a reef, there is an inexplicable pull to return once you have known Tahiti.

Marlon and I always remained close. We collaborated on two more master plans for Tetiaroa: one in 1983, after the hurricane, that included new sleeping huts for guests and a big house for Marlon, and another plan in 1998. None were ever implemented. We spent many enjoyable hours on the phone, in his Los Angeles bedroom, of course, and at my house. Marlon sought my advice on what to do with Tetiaroa until his death, and I was glad to give it. A short while before he died, Marlon decided against expanding his little hotel. He was investigating day tours in order to pay for much needed repairs. Potentially, guests would have arrived with well-prepared food and drink provided in Papeete, and would depart with the plane carrying the day's debris back. Days were to be spent enjoying the beaches, lagoon, and bird island with a guide. Marlon was at the same time working with Professor Edward Tarvid of Santa Monica College on negotiations with several university-sponsored environmental study programs for students to do research on the atoll.

When on the morning of July 1, 2004 Alice called to tell me that Marlon had died, I went into shock for many days. It was my wonderful wife, Blaine, who suggested I put my memories to paper lest the many rich stories of the development of Tetiaroa be forgotten.

I thank you, Marlon, wherever you are, for sharing your love of Tetiaroa with me, and for giving me the adventure of a lifetime. I left those reefs and those shoals a changed man. Never before and never since have I experienced anything quite like the splendor and captivating beauty of that tiny piece of our world.

Marlon in 1983, with a model of his dream house.

I wish to dedicate this book to Blaine, who understands that Tahiti and her islands have had a profound effect on my life. It was her inspiration that led me to write about my experiences on Tetiaroa. I extend my deepest appreciation to her for her unflinching support, and am thankful that she helped me change my incomprehensible grammar and sentence structure into something that could be read and understood. I also want to thank Helga Schier, my superb editor, who made me understand that a person reading a story also wants to know something about the person telling the story. I want to express my gratitude to Alice Marchak and Manutea Reasin, who both read the manuscript and made sure facts and dates were correct, and to Ann Poirer, Peggy and David Coats, and Ann Hughes, who each made many valuable suggestions. I'm equally indebted to Neil Ricklen, who worked his computer magic on my thirty-year-old slides. Silvia Utiger of Whitenoise, Los Angeles deserves kudos for her design input, as does Ann Videriksen, who introduced me to my publisher, Gordon Goff. I am forever grateful to Sara Pastrana for the beautiful design of the book.

In telling my story, I have left out many individuals who were integral to the process of creating the development on Tetiaroa, not the least of whom were members of Teai Taputuarai's construction crew. They were terrific. They worked hard while enduring many hardships on the atoll. I have omitted their numerous names in order to keep the narrative as concise as possible. I also wish to recognize the countless people who helped me out in those years. You know who you are, and I sincerely thank you for your invaluable contributions.

The photographs in this book were all taken by me unless attributed to Manutea Reasin (MR), Paul Faugerat collection (PF), Jenny Faugerat (JF), Rosette Valente (RV), Alice Marchak collection (AM), or Michele Darr (MD). I thank them for their help and generosity. I also wish to thank the Commune de Papeete for the use of photographs of the port of Papeete by C. Bosmel.

I am reminded that the past colors the present. Together they tell a story. It is not, however, the whole story.